MW01253371

PHILODEMUS, *ON PROPERTY MANAGEMENT*

Society of Biblical Literature

Writings from the Greco-Roman World

David Konstan and Johan C. Thom, General Editors

Editorial Board

Brian E. Daley
Erich S. Gruen
Wendy Mayer
Margaret M. Mitchell
Teresa Morgan
Ilaria L. E. Ramelli
Michael J. Roberts
Karin Schlapbach
James C. VanderKam

Number 33

PHILODEMUS, *ON PROPERTY MANAGEMENT*

PHILODEMUS,
ON PROPERTY MANAGEMENT

Translated with an introduction and notes by

Voula Tsouna

Society of Biblical Literature
Atlanta

PHILODEMUS, *ON PROPERTY MANAGEMENT*

Copyright © 2012 by the Society of Biblical Literature

Library of Congress Control Number: 2012952420

ISBN 978-1-58983-667-9 (paper binding : alk. paper)
ISBN 978-1-58983-765-2 (hardcover binding : alk. paper)

Printed on acid-free, recycled paper conforming to
ANSI/NISO Z39.48-1992 (R1997) and ISO 9706:1994
standards for paper permanence.

Contents

ACKNOWLEDGEMENTS

This volume has been many years in preparation. One reason was the parallel work that I had been doing on my book *The Ethics of Philodemus*, which contains material about the treatise *On Property Management*, and also on the French translation of *On Property Management* in collaboration with Daniel Delattre, which appeared in the recent volume *Les Épicuriens* in the series of La Bibliothèque de la Pléiade. Another reason why I took such a long time was that I found it difficult to strike a balance between a fully edited text and the kind of text I had agreed to produce for SBL. However, the present book has profited by the delay in so far as it has been informed by the research and the scholarly imput related to those other projects, and also in so far as the finished product is the outcome of many successive drafts of all its parts.

Elsewhere I have had the pleasure of acknowledging my intellectual debts to many Philodemus scholars in Europe and the United States with whom I have interacted during the last two decades. While I shall not mention them here by name, nonetheless I feel as obliged to them for their influence on the present monograph as I do for their help with my other contributions to Philodemean studies. On this occassion I wish especially to mention all those who have been directly involved in the preparation and the production of the volume at hand.

I thank Elisabeth Asmis and John Fitzgerald for their comments on the earliest draft and again John Fitzgerald for his criticisms on the latest version of the material. Kai Broder was so kind as to send me an electronic version of the Greek text, which subsequently served as the basis for the text printed in this volume. I am very grateful to him and also to Bob Buller for typesetting the new text and for integrating into it successive alterations and corrections.

I have presented material from this book at the University of Texas at Austin and at the University of Cambridge and wish to thank both audiences for their constructive remarks and criticisms. I am also pleased to acknowledge a sabbatical leave from the University of California at Santa Barbara in 2009–2010, which gave me the freedom from other academic duties needed to bring the project toward its completion. During the same period, I had the honor of holding an Onassis Foundation Fellowship, and I desire to thank the Foundation for its generous support.

My deepest gratitude is addressed to David Sedley and to David Konstan. In the capacity of academic editor, David Sedley provided me with searching criticisms and invaluable suggestions on several versions of the manuscript. Particularly important were his textual interventions, which resulted in new readings confirmed by the MSI and which are recorded at the foot of the relevant columns. David Konstan read and commented extensively on the penultimate version, leading to further substantial improvements. Moreover, as a co-editor of the SBL series (together with Johan Thom), he gave me constant encouragement and wise advice, always with characteristic courtesy and discretion.

I dedicate this book to my daughter, Eleni. May she come to see the wisdom of Philodemus's central idea, that the unrestrained pursuit of property and wealth is incompatible with the good life.

> I have a pretty child, like flowers
> of gold her form, my precious Cleis;
> whom I would not exchange
> for all of Lydia, or the lovely land.
> (Sappho 132, trans. West)

Athens, Greece, January 2011
VT

Abbreviations

Ad. contub.	Philodemus, [*Ad contubernales*] (*To Friends of the School*)
De div.	Philodemus, *De divitiis* (*On Wealth*)
De elect.	[Philodemus], [*De electionibus et fugis*] (*On Choices and Avoidances*)
De mort.	Philodemus, *De morte* (*On Death*)
De oec.	Philodemus, *De oeconomia* (*On Property Management*)
Ep. Men.	Epicurus, *Epistula ad Menoeceum* (*Letter to Menoeceus*)
Eth. nic.	Aristotle, *Ethica nicomachea* (*Nicomachean Ethics*)
Fact.	Valerius Maximus, *Factorum ac dictorum memorabilium libri IX* (*Memorable Deeds and Sayings in Nine Books*)
Gorg.	Plato, *Gorgias*
Hist.	*Historiae* (*Histories*)
Leg.	Plato, *Leges* (*Laws*)
Oec.	Xenophon, *Oeconomicus* (*On Property Management*)
Oeconomica	Theophrastus, *Oeconomica* (*On Property Management*)
Op.	Hesiod, *Opera et dies* (*Works and Days*)
Pol.	Aristotle, *Politica* (*Politics*)
Rhet.	Philodemus, *De rhetorica* (*On Rhetoric*)
Sent.	Epicurus, *Ratae sententiae* (*Key Doctrines*)
Symp.	Xenophon, *Symposium*
Vitae	Diogenes Laertius, *Vitae philosophorum* (*Lives of the Eminent Philosophers*)

INTRODUCTION

THE CONTENTS OF THE WORK

Philodemus is an important Epicurean philosopher of the first century B.C.E. (ca. 110–ca. 40 B.C.E.). Born in the city of Gadara in the Near East, he lived much of his life in Italy under the patronage of L. Calpurnius Piso and became the leader of a group of Epicureans located in one of Piso's country houses at the town of Herculaneum, in southern Italy. That town was completely destroyed by the volcanic eruption of Vesuvius in 79 C.E. In the mid-eighteenth century, archaeologists working in Herculaneum excavated the so-called Villa of the Papyri, which was plausibly identified with Piso's residence and whose library contained charred papyri with works by Philodemus.[1] Many of his writings treat ethical topics from the point of view of virtue ethics, and they make significant contributions to that field.

Philodemus's treatise entitled *On Property Management*, Περὶ οἰκονομίας (*De oec.*, PHerc. 1424),[2] constitutes the last part of the ninth, unusually well preserved book of his work *On Vices and the Opposite Virtues*, Περὶ κακιῶν καὶ τῶν ἀντικειμένων ἀρετῶν, a multivolume ensemble that discusses individual character traits, including arrogance and flattery. Thematically, *On Property Management*[3] is complemented by the writ-

---

1. See also below, pp. xli–xliii.

2. The text reprinted in this volume is Jensen 1906 with several new conjectures in the text and many modifications in punctuation (see also below, xliii). Laurenti 1973 contains an Italian translation and commentary on the treatise. Natali 1995 gives a survey of ancient philosophical approaches to οἰκονομία during the fourth century B.C.E. and the Hellenistic era. See also the edition and translation by Audring and Brodersen 2008.

3. Depending on the context, I usually render οἰκονομία as the management or administration of property, management or administration of the household, of one's estate, of wealth and property, of wealth and possessions, or of some combination

ing *On Wealth*, Περὶ πλούτου (*De div.*, PHerc. 163), of which only a few fragments survive.[4] By including it in a group of ethical writings dealing principally with character traits, Philodemus joins a long tradition of "economic" literature that flourished from the fourth century B.C.E. onward. Although οἰκονομία (transliterated *oikonomia*, property management) is not, strictly speaking, a virtue, it occupies a place in that tradition both because it crucially involves the exercise of the virtues and because it can be described as a disposition to have the right attitudes, beliefs, feelings, and so forth with regard to the possession and the administration of wealth. As such, οἰκονομία, according to Philodemus, is opposed to φιλοχρηματία, the love of money, the vice responsible for an excessive and harmful devotion to the pursuit of great wealth.[5] In the treatise *On Property Management*, Philodemus positions himself with regard to the "economic" tradition in two successive steps. In the first surviving part (frags. 1 and 2 and cols. A, B, and I.1–XII.2), he criticizes rival writings on property management, namely, the Οἰκονομικός (*Oec.*) of Xenophon and the first book of Pseudo-Aristotle's Οἰκονομικά (*Oeconomica*), which Philodemus attributes to Theophrastus.[6] In the second surviving part (XII.2–XXVIII.10), he defends his own views about the administration of property and wealth.

 On Property Management deserves our closest attention. It contains the most extensive treatment of οἰκονομία (property management) found in any Epicurean author, and, as will become obvious, it is more systematic and philosophical than rival approaches. It offers a thorough critique of the views of Xenophon and Theophrastus and gives us a better understanding of the moral issues generally pertaining to the acquisition

---

of the above. Occasionally I use "economics," "economic," or "financial" for οἰκονομία and its cognates. These terms take their meaning from the ancient theories that I discuss. They bear no relation to modern conceptions of economics as a theoretical field that involves the study of, for example, value, exchange, money, the organizational management of state revenues, and the like. Natali 1995 remarks that most ancient Greek uses of οἰκονομία preserve the core meaning of the good organization and management of a complex structure.

 4. The extant remains of the first book of *On Wealth* are edited by Tepedino-Guerra 1978.

 5. Alternatively, opposed to φιλοχρηματία is no single virtue but a cluster of virtues involved in the administration of property according to the principles of Epicurean philosophy.

 6. I shall henceforth refer to the author of the *Oeconomica* as Theophrastus, without prejudice to the question whether the attribution is correct.

and preservation of property and wealth. Philodemus asks, and gives a plausible answer to, a cluster of questions that ought to claim our interest: notably, whether the acquisition and maintenance of possessions are essential to our happiness, and to what extent our pursuit of these activities is compatible with the desire to live the good life.

1. TRADITIONAL APPROACHES TO PROPERTY MANAGEMENT: XENOPHON AND THEOPHRASTUS

Like the majority of ancient authors of treatises on οἰκονομία (property management), Xenophon and Theophrastus both take the administration of property and of the household (οἶκος, transliterated *oikos*) to be an art (οἰκονομικὴ τέχνη) with ethical and practical dimensions. In so far as it qualifies as such, property management is organized according to regulative principles, circumscribes a precise field of activity, and entails that the truly competent household manager is an expert in that field. Besides, in virtue of its technical character, it is believed to be teachable. The expert (οἰκονόμος, transliterated *oikonomos*) is in a position to transmit the general principles of the trade and can also give detailed instructions concerning the application of these principles to specific matters of economic practice. Teachings of this kind have a theoretical basis (θεωρία), in virtue of which they are put forward as pieces of advice about how to administer one's estate, supposedly delivered in a knowledgeable manner and with predictably good results.

In both theory and practice, property management is typically divided into four distinct domains, which correspond to four separate capacities of the expert in that art: the acquisition (κτῆσις), conservation (φυλακή), orderly arrangement (διακόσμησις), and use (χρῆσις) of possessions. The goal of each type of activity, and also of the art of property management as a whole, is to maximize profit and minimize loss (cf. "the more and the less"). In view of that goal, the good property manager perceives money-making (χρηματισμός) as a very important thing. One assumption that Xenophon and Theophrastus share is that there is no such thing as too much wealth. The more riches one can procure, the better it is, provided that they come through legitimate means and from socially acceptable sources. Another assumption that these authors make is that the property manager who is successful in greatly and rapidly increasing his estate is endowed with qualities and virtues that become manifest, precisely, in the exercise of his "economic" activities. On the contrary, a manager's failure to augment and preserve his estate reveals his shortcomings and vices. Generally, while Xenophon and Theophrastus include οἰκονομία (property management) among the most important occupations of a well-rounded life, neither of them recognizes that there are potential conflicts between the priorities set by property management and other priorities.

The broad picture emerging from Xenophon and Theophrastus, and generally from traditional treatises on property management, is an ambiguous one. On the one hand, they import ethical categories into the discussion of that field. On the other hand, by attributing to property management a considerable level of autonomy and by endorsing its goals and values as an art, they frequently seem to lose sight of its ethical relevance. The ambiguity is all the more problematic because οἰκονομία (property management) is perceived not only as an objective discipline, a τέχνη or ἐπιστήμη, but also as a stable state of mind (ἕξις), a form of practical wisdom (φρόνησις).[7] However, it is difficult to see how property management can coincide with a virtuous disposition, when the property manager gives preponderance to financial objectives above all others.[8] This tension constitutes the main focus of Philodemus's criticisms against both Xenophon and Theophrastus.

Xenophon's treatise Οἰκονομικός contains two different approaches to the topic of the administration of property, one philosophical, the other mundane. Socrates converses with Critoboulos, a wealthy Athenian who lives beyond his income and who seeks advice in order to remedy his situation. Socrates asks Critoboulos some questions. These help Critoboulos become clearer about the nature of his problem, but they also afford a glimpse into Socrates' own attitude toward property management, in particular the use and value of wealth. Subsequently, Socrates, who asserts that he is ignorant about the art of property management (*Oec.* 2.12–13), narrates the views of Ischomachus, a virtuous gentleman and an expert in that art. It is mainly from him that Critoboulos will learn what he wishes in a single lecture. The features of Xenophon's exposition that constitute the main targets of Philodemus's criticisms are the following. In the first phase of the conversation, Socrates induces his interlocutor to concede

---

7. See Natali 1995, 103.

8. The Stoics solve this problem by claiming that only the wise man is an expert in property management and only he possesses the relevant theoretical and practical disposition.

that the good property manager (ἀγαθὸς οἰκονόμος) should pursue what is useful or profitable (1.15). Whatever is profitable qualifies as wealth and possessions, whereas whatever is harmful is not wealth but loss. Hence the same things are wealth to those who understand how to use them but not wealth to those who do not (1.10). Money, but also friends, enemies, and possessions, are moral indifferents in that sense (1.12–15). Socrates calls "slaves of their passions" those people who have the required knowledge of οἰκονομία (property management) but are unwilling or unable to apply it to the administration of their own estates (1.19–20, 22–23). Although he does not consider Critoboulos one of them, he leads him to realize that he must strike a balance between his income and his needs (2.10). As to Socrates himself, he has found that balance (2.10). He calls himself rich because his small property of five minae is sufficient for his needs (2.2–3), while he calls Critoboulos poor for the opposite reason (2.2–8).

In the second phase of the conversation, Critoboulos learns from Ischomachus's account how to increase and administer his estate. Salient elements include the detailed instructions that Ischomachus gives to his wife about everything related to the household: how to distribute the income and regulate the expenses per month and per year; how to treat the servants; how to arrange things in the house so as to find them at a glance; how to choose a housekeeper and instill in her loyalty and justice; how to oblige her husband and her children "by the daily practice of the virtues" (7.43); and how to preserve her own natural beauty by going cheerfully about her many tasks. Husband and wife are equal partners in the pursuit of a common goal: "to act in such a manner that their possessions shall be in the best condition possible, and that as much as possible shall be added to them by fair and honorable means" (7.15). Similar instructions apply to the master of the estate. He personally chooses and trains the supervisors (ἐπίτροπος), teaching them justice; develops his ability to rule men, in particular his servants and slaves, whom he observes closely; is an expert in all aspects of the agricultural art; and so on. Again, Ischomachus claims that that kind of οἰκονομία (property management) is easy to learn and pleasant (6.9), gives beauty and health to the body, and removes most concerns of the mind (6.9–13). It also goes hand in hand with the possession of the virtues.[9]

---

9. Agriculture in particular, Ischomachus tells us, provides the surest test of good and bad men (*Oec.* 20.14).

As Philodemus remarks (*De oec.* VII.37–45), Theophrastus's account is heavily indebted to Xenophon's but makes additional claims as well. Theophrastus also treats οἰκονομία (property management) as an art and, moreover, compares it to the art of politics (cf. *Oeconomica* 1343a1–16).[10] He cites Hesiod's phrase "homestead first, and a woman; a plough-ox hardy to furrow"[11] to lend support to his own claim that the main components of the household are human beings and possessions, because the latter are essential to nourishment, whereas human beings are the first necessity for a free man (1343a18–23). Regarding the human part of the household, he argues that the relation between a man and his wife is both natural and beneficial and contributes greatly to one's happiness (1343b8–1344a8). He advises about the functions of the wife, the husband's treatment of her, the wife's virginity and habits of sexual intercourse, and her physical adornment. Also, he gives instructions as to how to procure and train both the supervisors of the property and the laborers (1344a23–b22), he regulates the correct apportionment of rewards or punishments, and he suggests ways in which slaves can be encouraged to be efficient.[12]

Like Xenophon, Theophrastus believes that another principal task of property management is to study the activities and arts by which one preserves and augments one's possessions (1343a23–26). The good

---

10. According to Theophrastus, οἰκονομία and politics differ in so far as they apply to different communities, the one to the οἶκος, the household, the other to the πόλις, the city-state, and also in so far as the government of the οἶκος is in the hands of one person, whereas that of the πόλις is entrusted to many people (1343a1–4). On the other hand, the two arts are similar to the extent that both are concerned with the making or the constitution of their objects, as well as with the use of them (1343a5–10). Theophrastus defines the πόλις in terms of "an assemblage of households, lands and possessions sufficient for living well" (1343a10–11) and infers from that that the οἶκος was formed before the πόλις and that, therefore, the art of household management is older than that of politics (1343a15–16).

11. Apparently the second half of the citation was not in the copy used by Philodemus. On this, see Armstrong 1935, 323–25.

12. For the purpose of understanding Philodemus's criticisms, note Theophrastus's recommendations that the master must not allow his slaves to be insolent nor, on the other hand, treat them with cruelty (1344a29–30); that he should give manual laborers abundant food but no wine at all; that he should hold festivals and give them treats; that he should avoid buying slaves who are either too cowardly or too spirited or who belong to the same nationality; and that he should encourage them to breed so as to keep their children and families as hostages for the slaves' fidelity.

property manager should be skillful in all four traditional domains of οἰκονομία (property management): acquisition, as much as preservation, arrangement, and use of goods (1344b22–28). He should make sure that the amount of fruitful possessions exceeds that of unfruitful ones, avoid risking all his possessions at once (1344b28–31), determine beforehand the monthly and yearly expenditures, and generally get personally involved in every aspect of the administration of his estate.[13] For present purposes, it is important to note that the master of the estate should periodically inspect all implements and stores and the orderly arrangement of utensils. Both he and his wife should rise before the servants and retire after them. Both should closely supervise in person their special department of household work. They should never leave their home unguarded, which might mean getting up in the middle of the night in order to watch over it. Finally, they should not postpone any of their tasks (1345a12–18). Like Xenophon, Theophrastus maintains that these habits preserve one's health and are also conducive to virtue (1345a13–14). The same holds for the principal and noblest sources of income: agriculture and farming. However, mining, trade, and the art of war are suitable sources of income as well (1343a26–31).

2. Philodemus's Criticisms against Xenophon and Theophrastus

Philodemus's criticisms address several different aspects of Xenophon's writing, and they vary in scope and strength. We may distinguish between two sets of objections, the one concerning Socrates, the other Ischomachus. The main objections against Socrates are that he distorts the ordinary meaning of terms related to property management, that what he says is vitiated by ambiguity, and that he shows himself to be naïve or even irrational.

At the outset, Philodemus clarifies that the primary function of property management, as it is ordinarily understood, is to govern well one's own home and the homes of others, "with 'well' taken to mean beneficially on a large and prosperous scale" (I.8–10). The person who possesses

---

13. Like Xenophon, Theophrastus is an admirer of the Persian and Spartan methods of property management, which require one's personal involvement in most aspects of the administration of one's estate. He also commends the Athenian method of selling and buying at the same time (1344b32–35, 1345a18–19).

the art of governing well will secure such benefits, live happily in his own home, and teach others how to do the same (cf. IIIa.6–16). Philodemus probably thinks that ordinary terms related to property administration, such as "wealth," "profit" or "benefit," "possessions," "poor" and "rich," "masters and slaves,"[14] and other related words, capture the usual and also the proleptic conception of property management and its functions, a conception based on προλήψεις (preconceptions), that is, fundamental notions derived from experience whose propositional content is always true.[15] Moreover, Philodemus seems to assume that so long as enquiry into these matters remains close to the relevant preconceptions, it will proceed smoothly and methodically and will lead to the truth. On the other hand, if one deviates from the familiar use of words, one is likely to ignore the corresponding preconceptions, conduct the investigation at random, and draw false inferences.

These are precisely the errors committed by Socrates.

[Although] ordinary language never uses [these names in this] way, this man crazily tries to deduce it from these names and forces it to have as masters, and as extremely wicked ones at that, the vices that act as hindrances, that is, idleness of the soul, carelessness, gambling, and inappropriate conversation, and turns those people who work and make [profits] for themselves but who [squander their household goods] into the [slaves of bad] masters—gluttony and drunkenness and ambition—things against which one must fight more than against [enemies]. (*De oec.* IV.1–16)

"Slaves" and "masters" refer to people in the household who have these respective positions and roles. By calling "slaves" the masters of an estate and "masters" the vices that afflict them, Socrates extends the ordinary meaning of the terms to a metaphorical meaning causing confusion.[16] A

---

14. Recall that traditional treatises on household management discuss these topics and that both Xenophon and Theophrastus explore the roles of and relationships between masters and slaves.

15. Since προλήψεις (preconceptions) are criteria of truth, ordinary language is a good (though not infallible) guide to the truth.

16. Philodemus does not object to metaphors as such. His point is probably that Socrates' metaphor is confusing, given the particular context in which it is used.

similar objection applies to Socrates' use of "possessions." On the basis of
the definition of an estate as everything that a person possesses (Xenophon, *Oec.* 1.5), Socrates infers, therefore, that one's estate also includes
the enemies that one possesses (1.7). On the other hand, in a fragmen-
tary passage Philodemus remarks that, if "to possess" is understood in
the principal sense, it refers to both the house and what one possesses
outside the house, but the verb does not have its principal sense in the
phrase "certain people possess enemies" (frag. I.19–21). The meaning that
Socrates lends to "poor" and "rich" is subject to similar criticisms (IV.29–
34). Calling rich a man whose entire estate is worth a small sum, but poor
someone whose property is worth a hundred times more, entails speaking "in a manner involving opinion ([δ]οξαστικῶς), not preconception
(οὐ προληπτικῶς) in accordance with ordinary usage" (V.2–4). Hence it is
likely to obstruct the proper order of investigation and lead to error.

A related charge is that the conversation between Socrates and Critoboulos is vitiated by ambiguity.[17] "They never yet [seem to assume] the
same meaning, because of [failure] to distinguish between different meanings" (*De oec.* VI.16–18). For instance, when Socrates says that he will
talk about property management (cf. VI.18–19), he means the balance
between his needs and his income, whereas Critoboulos has in mind the
optimal preservation and increase of his property. Yet another set of criticisms is that Socrates appears naïve, impractical, and even illogical. He
gives instructions about property management, although he has said that
he has not been taught that subject by anyone (see VI.11–20). He is always
out of touch with practical life (V.4–6). Further, some of his claims about
money and prosperity are downright crazy. "Besides, as regards his claim
that five minae seem to him sufficient for the necessary and natural needs
of men, that prosperity in life [is something empty], and that he does not
need anything more [in addition to those, it is impracticable and conflicts
with reason]" (V.6–14).

Of course, Xenophon could respond that, in fact, Socrates is aware
of his own shortcomings and therefore does not undertake himself to
teach Critoboulos but defers to Aspasia and especially to Ischomachus,
who are real experts in οἰκονομία (property management). Philodemus,
however, scores several points against Ischomachus as well, some of which

---

17. It is unclear whether Philodemus accuses Socrates of using ambiguity out of
intellectual dishonesty or merely out of confusion.

apply also to Theophrastus (see *De oec.* VII.37–45). He argues that several instructions issued by Xenophon and Theophrastus are trivial, others have no theoretical justification at all, and others are not applicable in practice. Moreover, many of their doctrines are either irrelevant to the subject matter of property management or incompatible with the philosophical life.

The theoretical pretensions of Xenophon and Theophrastus are punctured in several instances. "[It is easy for everyone] to learn the age [of horses and men, even if no deeper underlying theory is available]. Indeed, Critoboulos was aware of the fact, which is common knowledge, that some men have wives who act in a cooperative manner with the goal of increasing the property, whereas others have wives who act in a very damaging way" (*De oec.* II.1–8). Nor did Critoboulos need the aid of philosophy to learn things about farming, for that art "as a matter of fact derives from personal experience, not from philosophy" (VII.31–33). In fact, one wonders "who has been educated by the doctrines mentioned above, other than the person who has already approved of them" (VII.2–5). Theophrastus also makes trivial claims, for example, about the treatment of servants.

> The instructions concerning their [tasks], nourishment, and punishment are commonplace and observed by the more decent type of person, and they are not the special province of the philosopher. As to the precept that one should not use unreasonable methods of punishment, this does equally concern both theory and practice, but it should not have been taken up here in connection with the treatment of slaves. Otherwise, why should only this point be raised? (IX.44–X.7)

Besides, both Xenophon and Theophrastus advance positions that are arbitrary and lack theoretical support. For instance, there is no good reason to suppose that agriculture is in accordance with nature, that it constitutes the first and best source of income, or that mining and other similar activities are suitable for the good person (VIII.40–45). Nor should one accept without argument Theophrastus's assertions that the house is the principal element of nourishment and the woman the principal element of free men (VIII.32–40). Equally unjustified are Theophrastus's instructions about the way to approach one's wife (IX.4–5), about marrying a virgin (IX.8–9), about the paramount importance of slaves (IX.9–13), and about the recruitment, training, and distribution of tasks in the household to different kinds of servants (IX.13–26). Furthermore, Philodemus questions the practical applicability of Ischomachus's doctrines, in particular with regard to moral matters. Ischomachus does not make clear how one can teach the servants not to steal, let alone how one can develop in the property manager the capacity of making people just (VII.16–26). Ischomachus's idea that the good estate manager knows enough to be completely self-sufficient and does not need any advice is also unsound. "To posit that (beyond what he himself knows his bailiff) has no need of anything else I consider the mark of a fool" (VII.1–2).

Many of these elements fall outside the proper scope of οἰκονομία (property management). For instance, this holds for the analogy that Theophrastus draws between property management and politics, which, according to Philodemus, is both irrelevant and untenable (VII.45–VIII.24).[18] On the other hand, features that do belong to traditional property management are indifferent or harmful to the person who wishes to live the philosophical life. Both Xenophon and Theophrastus prescribe the activities pertaining to property management according to the Persian, Spartan, Libyan, and Attic methods (De oec. A.11–27, B.11–18),[19] in particular according to the fourfold division of the activities of the οἰκονόμος (property manager) mentioned above. By contrast, Philodemus contends that, of the four traditional domains of property management, the one that is truly useful for the philosopher is the preservation of possessions. Also, while Theophrastus recommends that the tasks of property management should be distributed in such a way as to avoid endangering all of the property at once, Philodemus replies as follows: "Of course, (this) is good advice for an ordinary person. But the philosopher, properly speaking, does not work, nor, if he ever works, does he seem to put everything at risk so as [to need exhortation] not to do it" (XI.11–21). The meticulous arrangement of possessions is central to the Persian method (A.18–20) and strongly recommended by Ischomachus and Theophrastus; Philodemus, however, views it as a waste of time.

---

18. Philodemus seems to concede that οἰκονομία and politics are both arts. The Epicurean will not practice either of them as art, and while, as we shall see, he will practice οἰκονομία nontechnically, he will not practice politics at all.

19. See notes 2–6, 8, and 36.

Particularly interesting are Philodemus's criticisms of the importance that Xenophon and Theophrastus attribute to the wife. First, while they maintain that it is natural and useful to take a wife, Philodemus denies that she is important to the philosopher's happiness. Even if she contributes as much as her husband to the material prosperity of the estate, she is not necessary to one's happiness, if one is a philosophically inclined man (*De oec.* II.8–36). Second, Philodemus appears to object to Theophrastus on hermeneutical and logical grounds.[20] He concedes that Theophrastus's analytic examination of the two parts of the household belongs, on the face of it, to the subject of property management. Nonetheless, he considers mistaken Theophrastus's interpretation of Hesiod's division of the household into two parts, humans and possessions, mainly because of inconsistencies related to the theses that the wife is necessary to the free man and that she is an equal partner in the household. "It is worthwhile to enquire further how (Theophrastus) adds to these remarks that 'consequently, according to Hesiod, it would be necessary that "first and foremost there is a house and a woman," because the one is the principal element of [nourishment] while the other of [free men],' unless the wife is a possession just like food despite being a partner in the management of the household" (VIII.24–32). It seems, then, that Hesiod's phrase cannot be used to support the distinction of the primary parts of the household into human beings and possessions or Theophrastus's justification of it. I am unclear as to just what Philodemus's argument is here, but I think that it runs along the following lines. Theophrastus maintains that the wife is necessary to the free man in a sense analogous to that in which the possession of an estate is necessary to nourishment. This entails that the wife is a possession of some sort, while Hesiod's twofold division of the household into a house (or estate, more broadly) and a woman implies that the wife is something different from mere possessions. Besides, Theophrastus seems to contradict himself. For on the one hand, in the analogy mentioned above, he treats the wife, a human being, in terms of something that the free man needs and gets, that is, a possession. On the other hand, he claims also that the household consists of human beings and possessions, and thus he classifies the wife as a human being, not a possession.

---

20. Although this objection may appear tedious, in fact it is difficult to reconstruct it, especially because there is no secondary literature on the relevant passage. Therefore I shall discuss that passage in some detail.

Further tension is caused by Theophrastus's view of the wife as an equal partner in the administration of the household. For if she is a possession, just like victuals are, she cannot be her husband's equal. So, it would seem that, in order to be consistent, Theophrastus would have to drop either the belief in the equality of the spouses or the distinction between two parts of the household, as well as the reasons that he gives in defense of it. In fact, we saw that Philodemus calls arbitrary the contention that the woman is the principal element of free men (VIII.34–35). Subsequently, he argues that this claim is simply not true. "(It is worthwhile to examine) [why], of the preoccupations of the household that deal with people, he assumes the one concerning the wife to be first and foremost, given that there can be a happy life even without her" (VIII.46–IX.3).

Concerning the care of servants and slaves, Philodemus rejects many of his rivals' views because he finds them harsh and even inhumane. Notably, he denounces Theophrastus's claims that no wine should be given to the slaves (IX.26–44) and that the master should bind his slaves to his service by holding their wives and children as hostages, which Philodemus considers even harsher than Xenophon's advice to raise the children of one's good servants but not of the bad ones (X.15–21). On the other hand, he also finds objectionable Theophrastus's instruction that the master should cater to the pleasure and entertainment of his servants, going to considerable trouble and expense for that purpose (X.21–28), for presumably this instruction entails more toils than benefits for the master, and it promotes the servants' pleasure rather than his own.

More generally, Philodemus's view is that the assiduous personal involvement of the property manager in every aspect of the administration of the estate involves practices "wretched and unfitting for the philosopher" (XI.30–31). Habits such as getting up in the course of the night reveal mistakes in the hedonistic calculus: they require toils that outweigh pleasures and therefore hinder our attainment of the moral end.[21]

---

21. Philodemus maintains that getting up in the course of the night, especially when the nights are short, is damaging to health as well as to the study of philosophy (XI.38–41). Contrast the pattern of Ischomachus's life, which lends support to the suggestion that hard work is conducive to health and well-being. Ischomachus trains his wife and supervises her doings; thinks a great deal about the building and furnishings of his house and the layout of its contents; selects and constantly checks his servants, housekeeper, and supervisors; rises early, walks to his farm, superintends all the details of farm work, runs back home, has lunch, and returns to work right

A few more criticisms ought to be mentioned. Philodemus accuses Xenophon of introducing Ischomachus not only as a good property manager but also as a man of practical wisdom and virtue (VI.3–8), whereas he says or does things unworthy of such a man. The immediate context does not reveal just what these things are (see VI.1–3), but it seems likely that they are dictated by the goals of οἰκονομία, that is, property management, in which Ischomachus is an expert. Not only are they unphilosophical, but they may derive from vice. Moreover, Philodemus complains that the "cosmetic" part of property management does not take its place beside acquisition and preservation in the art of property management, if arranging things in the proper way and place is understood under "cosmetic," but he does allow Xenophon to prescribe the kind of arrangement that adds pleasure to the useful part of the province of the manager (X.39–XI.3). Subsequently, he makes the point that "it is the mark of a mercenary person to advise having a greater quantity of 'fruitful' than of 'unfruitful' possessions—if, at any rate, by these (Xenophon) meant lucrative and unlucrative. For if instead he meant useful and useless in general, he should have recommended that everything should be useful and nothing useless" (XI.3–11).

The dialectical part of the treatise *On Property Management* ends near the beginning of column XII (XII.2). Philodemus, however, elaborates the above objections further in the expository part of the work, in particular in the systematic contrast that he draws between the traditional property manager and the Epicurean property manager, who aspires to live the philosophical life.

---

afterward; puts an enormous amount of care and toil into the cultivation of his fields; and so on. The duties that he prescribes for his wife are no less cumbersome. She must receive the income, distribute as much of it as must be spent, and save the rest; regulate the expenses of the household per month and per year; make sure that the goods are properly stored or used; supervise, instruct, correct, reward or punish, and care for the servants, thus increasing their market value; and oblige her husband and her children "by the daily practice of the virtues' (*Oec.* 7.43). Furthermore, she should arrange things in the house so that "a glance will reveal anything that wants attention, and the knowledge of where each thing is will quickly bring it to hand so that we can easily use it" (8.10). She must choose the housekeeper and instill in her the virtues, notably loyalty and justice. She must attend to the possessions herself, if she wishes to have optimal results. If Ischomachus is to be believed, all this labor will help her preserve her physical beauty better than any cosmetics might.

3. Philodemus's Approach to Property Management and the
Debate between the Epicureans and the Cynics

"We shall discuss, then, not how one can live well at home, but what
attitude one must take up both with regard to the acquisition and the
preservation of wealth, concerning which property management and the
property-management expert are in fact conceived specifically, (and we
shall do so) without contending at all with those who prefer to make other
meanings underlie the terms and, moreover, discussing the acquisition (of
property) that is appropriate for the philosopher, [not] for just anyone"
(De oec. XII.5–17). This passage contains certain programmatic remarks
that circumscribe the scope of Philodemus's approach to οἰκονομία (property management) and define the nature of his subject. Unlike Xenophon
and Theophrastus, he will narrow down the scope of his treatment of
οἰκονομία and its practitioners. First, he announces, he will not discuss
property management in terms of a general ethical subject pertaining to
both public and private aspects of daily life. Rather, he will concentrate
on the specifically economic tasks of acquisition (κτῆσις) and preservation (φυλακή) of property on the assumption that these are, in truth, the
principal activities indicated by the ordinary use of οἰκονομία (property
management) and its cognates. Moreover, he will abstain from verbal or
semantic debates concerning the ordinary and the technical meanings of
such terms. His purpose is not to survey various definitions of property
management and other related concepts but rather to examine the main
activities involved in estate management and our moral attitudes toward
them. Principally, he will address neither the gentleman nor the layman
but the philosopher broadly conceived, namely, anyone minded to live
according to the principles of the Epicurean doctrine. Further, he will
not be concerned with limitless wealth but only with a proper measure of
wealth as well as the philosopher's capacity for managing it. These restrictions place Philodemus's discussion of Epicurean property management
on the right philosophical footing. It does not bear on the pragmatics of
the household nor on ways and means of becoming and remaining rich.
Chiefly, it aims to determine how and to what extent people who desire
to live the philosophical life can engage in property management without compromising their ethical principles or endangering their happiness.
The last restriction in particular bears on the objection that the philosopher should not have any property to administer but should provide for
his rudimentary needs on a day-to-day basis. Philodemus addresses that

objection by drawing on an older debate between Metrodorus and the Cynics, who had proposed that the philosopher should live in utter poverty in order to be carefree (see XII.29–XIV.23).

According to Philodemus, Cynics and Epicureans agree that the best life is free from toil and worry but disagree as to how it can be attained, especially in respect of the possession and administration of wealth. On the one hand, the Cynics advocate a beggarly lifestyle for the reason that wealth is troublesome and, therefore, harmful to one's peace of mind. On the other hand, Metrodorus maintains that a peaceful and happy life is obtained not by avoiding all toils and efforts but by opting for things that may involve a certain amount of trouble at present but relieve us of much greater concerns in the future. Wealth is such a thing, as are health and friendship. Although its possession and administration doubtless requires thought and labor, it is better to have it than not, for its presence allows the virtuous man to live pleasantly, whereas its absence is responsible for deprivation and distress. The only way in which the Cynics might be able to establish that the possession of natural wealth (φυσικὸς πλοῦτος, XIV.19)[22] is less preferable to the daily provision of goods would be to prove that, in fact, the former entails more pains and efforts than the latter. However, following Metrodorus's line, Philodemus suggests that it is highly unlikely that such a proof would be forthcoming. One practical implication of the Epicurean position is that the good person should not reject as useless the wealth that may come his way. The entire argument is based on the rational calculation of pleasures and pains and also makes use of the concept of natural wealth, which is related to the concept of the measure of wealth (πλούτου μέτρον).[23] Since Philodemus's presentation of Epicurean οἰκονομία (property management) involves both these notions, I shall explain them briefly.

In outline, natural wealth is one of the many objects that we naturally seek in order to satisfy natural desires and thus feel pleasure. In so far as this kind of desire has a limit, natural wealth also has a limit, and, besides, it is easy to obtain (Epicurus, *Sent.* 15) precisely because it is natural (Epicurus, *Ep. Men.* 130).[24] Correspondingly, the measure of wealth that is appropriate for the philosopher covers the range of the philoso-

---

22. See note 38.
23. See notes 38 and 39.
24. See note 54.

pher's natural needs. "There is for the philosopher a measure of wealth that, [following] the founders of the school, we have passed down in [the treatise] *On Wealth*, resulting in an account of the capacity to administer the acquisition of this and the preservation of this" (XII.17–25). Further, in so far as the measure of wealth satisfies the philosopher's natural needs, it is slightly superior (*De div.* LI.27–30) or, from another perspective (see *De oec.* XIV.9–23), clearly preferable to poverty. In fact, there is tension in Philodemus's position. On the one hand, he emphasizes the instrumental importance of wealth and its administration for the good life. On the other hand, following the authorities of the school, he holds on to the view that the difference between possessing and lacking wealth, and between preserving it and not preserving it, is but small (XVIII.25–31), and he suggests that the superiority of wealth is mainly practical rather than moral. Roughly, the position that he maintains is the following. "More" wealth may be better than "less," because of the serenity and the material comforts that it affords when it is correctly used. Further, "more" wealth can be interpreted in many ways, since Philodemus does not fix precisely how much money and possessions are optimal for the philosophical life. On the other hand, "more" corresponds somehow to "the measure of wealth" but never amounts to the open-ended goal of traditional οἰκονομία, namely, to amass as many riches as possible through decent and lawful means.

Recall that Xenophon and Theophrastus postulate that the administration of property constitutes a domain in which its practitioners manifest important features of their personality and character and, notably, virtues and vices. Philodemus also shares that view, and he bolsters his own position about property management by contrasting two kinds of property manager: the traditional οἰκονόμος (property manager); and the philosophically minded manager who acts according to the principles laid down by Epicurus.

Philodemus describes the right approach to property management in terms of a certain easy attitude required of the philosopher toward the acquisition and preservation of possessions and specifies that attitude by referring to the elements deriving from the philosopher's disposition and beliefs. Notably, the philosopher should not care too much about the goal of traditional property management, the more and the less, but should cultivate some kind of emotional detachment with regard to his gains and losses (*De oec.* XIV.23–XV.3). He should be able to do so in great part because he holds true beliefs (or knowledge), first of all, about the nature of our desires and inclinations. He correctly believes that "there are within us natural [desires] for more goods" (XVI.30–31), on account of which we should choose to preserve our wealth in so far as no unseemly labor is involved (XVI.25–28). But he is also convinced that wealth has no intrinsic value and that he can live happily without it (see XV.31–XVI.18). What makes it possible for the philosopher to feel and act in such a way is, indeed, his confidence that Epicurus was right in saying that natural and necessary desires are easy to satisfy and that their fulfillment is all that the philosopher needs in order to pursue his way of life. At the same time, as mentioned, he has a correct appreciation of the instrumental value of wealth, which motivates his efforts as a property manager and is related to his natural inclination toward "more goods' (cf. XVI.30–31). In fact, if the philosopher acquires more possessions than he had before, he should accept them, provided that they come to him in a blameless and effortless manner (XVI.44–46).[25] Generally speaking, he holds true beliefs about what is and is not profitable and makes choices accordingly (XIII.20–23).

Dispositional elements underlie the philosopher's property management also in so far as he provides for the needs of his fellow Epicureans and makes some of his wealth available to his friends. In particular, Philodemus mentions in many places the philosopher's attitudes of goodwill, benevolence, and gratitude; his generosity and philanthropy; and his thorough appreciation of the value of friendship. The text may or may not contain references to donations that the philosophical property manager makes to the Epicurean school, to communal administration, or to both. For example, "one's readiness to share things very much on one's own initiative" (XV.2–3) may or may not allude to regular contributions to the Epicurean community. Also, Philodemus's statement, that the Epicurean manager is capable of exhorting men "to share all their wealth (freely) inspired by his confidence in the adequacy of few possessions and assisted by the discourses of the sage" (XVIII.4–7), can be taken to imply a reference to communal administration but does not need to be read in that way. In any case, Philodemus's thesis is not merely that the easy attitude of the sage toward the administration of wealth is *compatible* with having friends but that it is in part *shaped* by their presence or absence. "That the wise man administers these goods in such a manner is a consequence of

---

25. In this respect, Philodemus's approach to οἰκονομία accommodates his audience, which is partly constituted by very wealthy Roman patricians, including Philodemus's patron Piso.

the fact that he has acquired and continues to acquire friends" (XV.3–6). Their needs and pleasures figure prominently in his calculations concerning his monthly and yearly expenses, the distribution of his income, and the manner in which he provides for the future.

Thus the Epicurean οἰκονόμος (property manager) spends money carefully and in proportion to his income (XXV.23–24) without, however, acting like a miser. He keeps flexible the amounts that he spends per month and per year, as well as the ways in which he allocates his income to different things (XXV.31–42), because he occasionally wishes to spend much more than usual on his friends or because the circumstances and his sense of decorum sometimes guide him to offer gifts rather than to buy furnishings for his house or store up his belongings (XXV.42–XXVI.1). When he needs to retrench in his expenses, he makes sure that the cuts are not excessive or undignified and that they primarily affect him rather than his friends (XXVI.1–9).[26] Moreover, the claims of friendship determine the extent to which he needs to save and make provision for the future. "If one has friends, one should save more in order that they may have [means of maintaining themselves] even after one's death, and one should regard them as one's children. On the other hand, if one does not have friends, [one should relax] not only the practice of saving money but also the more parsimonious management of property" (XXVII.5–12). Generally speaking, the philosopher acts in these matters "like those who sow seeds in the earth" (XXV.17–18). What he spends on his friends represents a more profitable acquisition than lands (XXV.2–3) and enables him to reap many times more fruits in the future (XXV.16–23). In that sense, caring for one's friends entails also providing for one's own future (XXV.11–12). "This strategy both gives us good hopes right now and, when it comes to be present, it makes us happy" (XXV.12–14). As Hermarchus said, it is the treasure that is most secure against the turns of fortune (XXV.3–4).

As to the virtues, the Epicurean property manager is free of greed, the principal vice related to wealth, but possesses the virtue standing opposite to greed, which is not identified in the treatise. We could determine it in negative terms, as the absence of greed or of the love of money (ἀφιλοχρηματία).[27] Alternatively, we might identify it as οἰκονομία (prop-

---

26. See note 75.
27. The term does exist in the Greek language, although authors rarely use it.

erty management), since Philodemus opposes the good οἰκονόμος, the good property manager, to the φιλοχρήματος, the lover of money (XVII.2–14). In any case, that virtue is found together with social virtues, namely, liberality, goodwill, gratitude, and the willingness to return favors, and also coexists with one's disposition to make and keep friends. Additional virtues are manifested in the relationships of the Epicurean manager to his subordinates, especially servants and slaves: mildness of character, sensitivity, humanity, philanthropy, and decency (cf. IX.32; X.15–21; XXIII.4–5, 20–22). We shall see below that he expresses his gratitude to the sages who have instructed him by offering them gifts (XXIII.27–29), and if he himself is a teacher, he gracefully accepts the gifts of his students (XXIII.30–32). His inclination to ask other people for practical advice indicates that he is not afflicted by arrogance and presumption (XXVI.24–28), and his manner of regulating expenditure shows generosity as well as moderation and prudence. Finally, the philosopher does not suffer from the vices that obstruct putting one's desires and fears in good order[28] but possesses precisely the virtues that contribute to the successful preservation of his property (XXIII.36–XXIV.19). He has moderation in his lifestyle, temperance in respect of physical pleasure, modesty and unaffected manners, fortitude with regard to pain, and justice. He does not fear the gods or death and does not suffer from the vices connected with such fears.[29] In short, he cultivates all the major virtues in practicing οἰκονομία (property management) in the belief that to do so is both morally good and financially expedient.

In sharp contrast, the traditional property manager, whom Philodemus describes as an expert,[30] sets it as his goal to have as many gains and as few losses as possible and increase his property to the greatest extent possible by honorable means. The writings of Xenophon and Theophrastus highlight the fact that the expert manager is intensely involved in all four types of activities related to his art (acquisition, preservation, arrangement, and use) but attribute the greatest importance to the acquisition of money and possessions. Comparably to the case of the Epicurean property manager, Philodemus describes the expert's approach to

---

28. The idea seems to be that vices are closely related to unruly desires and fears, which drive one to the pursuit of valueless and harmful things; many of these things have to do with the aggressive acquisition and possession of great wealth.

29. See also *De elect.* XXI.2–XXIII.13. Philodemus is probably the author of that work.

30. See below, pp. xxx–xxxiii.

property management mainly in terms of a certain disposition and of the feelings, attitudes, beliefs, and character traits characteristic of that disposition. In addition, he mentions specific practices dictated by the expert's single-minded pursuit of wealth and indicates how they are harmful.

Unlike the philosopher, the traditional οἰκονόμος (property management) is not easygoing concerning matters of his art. He develops "an obsessive [zeal] concerning the more and the less" (De oec. XIV.26–27), in virtue of which he is willing to subject himself to grave troubles and the heaviest labors. Because of his zeal, he is very much distressed about his losses and is elated about his gains (cf. XIV.23–25). Trying to maximize his revenues, he often puts all of his eggs in one basket, either by distributing financial tasks in certain ways (XI.11–14) or by investing in possessions belonging only to one kind (XXVI.34–39). These practices lead him to endanger all of his property at once, sometimes reducing himself "to utter poverty" (XXVI.38–39.). More generally, his excessive attachment to the goal of "the more and the less" is responsible for the practical and emotional instability of his life. He makes himself vulnerable to extreme changes of fortune and is also racked by violent emotions, including anxiety and fear about the future. These drawbacks are increased by the fact that the traditional manager has no true friends. Further, he could not have any, since, according to Philodemus, he perceives friends as obstacles to his primary goal, the maximal growth and efficient administration of his estate (XXIV.41–46). Also, the expert manager is indifferent to the calls of society and to the sufferings of other human beings. He resists paying visits to people (XXVI.9) and does not mind making money from his slaves' forced labor in mines (XXIII.4–5).

The expert manager's obsession with wealth is dictated by empty beliefs and the endorsement of worldly values. Unlike the Epicurean manager, he confuses the natural desire for more goods with nonnatural desires whose satisfaction requires great wealth. He sees that kind of wealth as fundamental to his well-being. He considers profitable only what contributes to "the more and the less" and unprofitable the opposite. As we shall see, he ranks highly the sources of income that bring glory or spectacular gains without calculating how much toil and trouble they may involve for himself or for others. Philodemus suggests that such beliefs lead the expert manager to make mistakes in the performance of hedonistic calculations, for example, to judge that the absence of friends is more profitable than their presence. In sum, he lives a life full of concerns, hard work, tension and fear, sudden changes, and personal and social loneliness.

Unlike the Epicurean property manager, the traditional property manager exhibits major vices in pursuing his tasks. The central one is probably the love of money or greed. In addition, Philodemus's criticisms of Xenophon and Theophrastus indicate that the traditional manager is affected by arrogance and stupidity (*De oec*. VII.2), presumption (VII.21–26), harshness (IX.32) and inhumanity (X.15–21), possibly imprudence (XI.11–16), and certainly folly. Philodemus mentions these vices in the second part of his treatise and adds also to the list several other faults of character. Greed is often accompanied by avarice, insensitivity, ingratitude, and a lack of generosity and goodwill. These traits are responsible for the fact that the traditional manager tends to live a friendless life (ἀφιλία, XXIV.20). Moreover, deriving one's income from a military career betrays vain glory and a lack of wisdom (XXII.24), deciding to practice the art of horsemanship is dictated by similar traits, and getting revenues from the work of slaves in mines (XXIII.4–5) in most circumstances shows lack of humanity and callousness.

Besides, Philodemus asserts that certain vices hinder the correct management of one's desires and fears.[31]

Of the recommended activities leading to profits and the maintenance both of these and of the possessions that one had beforehand, one must keep in mind that the principal one consists in managing one's desires and fears. For, [usually], nothing drains and ruins the most illustrious and [richest houses] so much as [extravagance in lifestyle], lechery, ostentatious actions, [effeminate behavior], and similar things and, again, the chilling fear of the gods, of death, of pains and of the things that are believed to produce them. Consequently, if one removes from oneself, to the extent that it is possible, the envy of things that are not to be envied and the fear of things that are not to be feared, one will be able both to procure and to preserve (one's property) in the appropriate manner. Injustice, too, is thought to bring about each one of these things (sc. the acquisition and preservation of property), but, in fact, afterwards it takes away the greatest part not just of what one has gained but also of what one has had beforehand. It follows that, if one actually practices

---

31. See note 68.

justice, one will both obtain and safeguard the gain acquired in conformity with it. (XXIII.36–XXIV.19)

Philodemus completes his argument by claiming that every major fault of character is bound to affect one's attitudes toward property management and by emphasizing in that manner the close relation between οἰκονομία (property management) and ethics. "Indeed, I believe that absolutely every vice raises obstacles to the pleasant collection and to the maintenance of one's possessions, whereas their opposite virtues contribute considerably to them" (XXIV.35–40).

4. The Epicurean Philosopher as a Property Manager

However, Philodemus appears to entertain the following objection. Precisely because the Epicurean property manager administers his estate according to philosophical priorities, he is a bad manager, or at least a worse manager, than the expert in all four domains of property management, namely, the acquisition, preservation, arrangement, and use of wealth. While the traditional or expert manager assiduously concerns himself with "the more and the less," the Epicurean administrator gets sidetracked by ethical considerations and does not aim at the maximal increase of his property. Moreover, virtues such as generosity, philanthropy, and the disposition to care for one's friends are morally desirable, but they harm the growth and preservation of one's estate in ways in which their corresponding vices do not.

Philodemus's response to this charge is complex and ingenious. In the first place, he points out that the philosopher cannot reasonably be called a bad manager in the ordinary sense of the term. On the one hand, regarding the acquisition and preservation of great sums of money, the philosopher falls short of being an efficient manager in the ordinary sense, for "he will not be able to acquire a very large quantity of possessions and in a very short time" (XIX.4–5), and even if he does, it will not be easy for him to keep it (XVIII.37–39). "Nor (will he be able) to examine closely in what manner the greater part of his possessions could increase as much as possible" (XIX.4–7), since he does not measure them according to financial criteria (XIX.7–12). Nor yet will he be able to watch always with eagerness over the possessions that he already has, because this would require a level of worry and effort that he does not deem worth his while (XIX.10–23).

On the other hand, at least in so far as estates of reasonable size are concerned, the philosopher cannot be called a bad manager (XVI.21–25), for he does not waste his wealth but preserves it. Also, a bad manager is not successful in his activities, whereas the Epicurean administrator is. He will not fail "[if he administers] his estate with ease by aid of [reason] itself and of the [common] experience that is adequate for the management of one's possessions, though not for excessive moneymaking" (XVI.32–39).

In the second place, the preconception (πρόληψις) of the good money-maker (ἀγαθὸς χρηματιστής) points to the sage as the ideal moneymaker. Consider the following passage.

> We must not, on the other hand, [violate] this (sc. the meaning of the expression "the good moneymaker") through [the ordinary usage] of linguistic expressions, as sophists do, especially as we would be showing nothing about the acquisition and use (of wealth) pertaining to the wise man. Rather, we must refer to the preconception that we possess about a good moneymaker, ask in whom the content of that preconception is substantiated and in what manner that person makes money, and ascribe the predicate "good moneymaker" [to whomever it may be in whom] those features are attested. For just this reason, if we want to claim that, in the preconception, the good moneymaker is the one who acquires and takes care of wealth in accordance with what is advantageous, then we must proclaim that the sage above all is such a man. But if, on the other hand, in the preconception, we apply the quality of the good moneymaker rather to the man [who obtains for himself] many possessions with ability and expertise, and also not in a dishonorable way but lawfully, however much it may be true that [in this mode of acquisition] he encounters more sufferings than pleasures, then we must affirm that it is people other than sages who belong to that category (sc. of good moneymakers). (XX.1–32)[32]

Philodemus recognizes that the expression "the good moneymaker" is ambiguous and that the relevant preconception can be developed in two different ways, one attaching the property of the good moneymaker to a

---

32. See note 57.

good person, the other attaching it to a person who is good at making a maximal amount of money by legitimate means. However, Philodemus relies on the clarity and the criterial power of the preconception in order to unpack the πρόληψις (preconception) of the good moneymaker in the right way: it is instantiated in the philosopher, not in the expert, as many people think.

In the third place, Philodemus defends the distinction between the expert property manager and the philosopher, drawing a clear line where the philosopher's involvement with οἰκονομία (property management) ought to stop:

> Thus, the wise man perhaps cannot be called in equal measure at one and the same time an expert (τεχνίτης) and a producer of possessions (ἐργάτης) collected in great quantity and in a short time. For in fact there is an empirical practice (ἐμπειρία) and ability (δύναμις) specially related to moneymaking, too, of which a good man will not have a share, nor will he watch the opportunities in combination with which even this kind of ability could be useful. For all these things characterize the person who loves money. Nevertheless, (what holds in this case) at any rate appears to be exactly like what holds in the case of several other practices in which, although there exist good professional workmen, each one of us could accomplish quite well, as it were, at least what is sufficient for our needs. We observe this, for example, in the production of bread or in the preparation of food. For everybody is able to make such things for himself to the point of meeting sufficient needs, although there is an empirical practice involving expertise [about] them as well. Now, it seems that something like this holds also regarding the acquisition and preservation of property. For even if we are not, like certain people, experts in amassing and preserving wealth nor earnest and persevering managers of property, [nonetheless] there seem to be many persons who are not bad at this, at least to the point of finding what they need and not [totally] failing in this matter by acting randomly. The good man, too, must be counted among these people. (XVII.2–40).

Philodemus concedes, once again, that there is such a thing as the τέχνη of οἰκονομία (the art of property management) and that there exist experts in that field. On the other hand, he asserts that the philosopher does not possess the art in question, nor does he qualify as an expert in that sense. The main criterion, then, according to which he distinguishes the ordinary manager from the philosopher seems to be cognitive: the former possesses a form of knowledge, an art or τέχνη, that the latter does not possess. It seems reasonably clear that here "art" (τέχνη) is not a strictly rationalistic concept but involves experience as well as theory. In fact, in this work Philodemus generally uses τέχνη as an equivalent to ἐμπειρία or ἔντεχνος ἐμπειρία, that is, an empirical activity involving expertise or artful practice.[33] Thus he describes the expert (τεχνίτης) in terms of the man who has the practical ability to achieve certain results in a regular and knowledgeable manner, rather than conjecturally and at random.[34] In the case at hand, the expert (τεχνίτης) in moneymaking has the ability to gain and preserve money in a certain and predictable way, comparable to that of craftsmen in practical knacks such as breadmaking. On that conception, an art (τέχνη) has theoretical dimensions as well. These mainly consist in the systematization of a body of knowledge according to certain principles or rules and in the attainment of the goal of the art (τέχνη) through their regular application. The contents of Xenophon's and Theophrastus's works give us a glimpse into the regulative principles of property management, and we find in Ischomachus an excellent instantiation of a τεχνίτης, an expert, in that art.

On the other hand, Ischomachus can equally well be taken to represent what the philosopher most emphatically will *not* be. The philosopher will not conduct the administration of his property in a technical manner but will rely instead on common experience accompanied by reason (see XVI.34–35), for these suffice to secure the financial means to a stable and tranquil life (XIV.46–XV.1). The reason why the philosopher will always resist becoming an expert in the administration of property is found in the following passage. "It is not, then, disagreeable that there should sometimes be another person of this kind, in the role of a servant, just like the expert in the production of bread. But that he himself (sc. the true philosopher) should be a producer of such things is inappropriate.

---

33. See Tsouna-McKirahan 1996, especially 710. On the Epicurean concept of τέχνη and the distinctions pertaining to it, see Blank 1995.

34. See Philodemus's definition of τέχνη in *Rhet.* 2, PHerc. 1674 XXXVIII.5–19; Longo Auricchio 1977, 123. The text is translated and discussed by Blank 1995, 179.

For this kind of acquisition, when measured against toil, is no longer profitable" (XIX.23–32). Ultimately, the expertise of the ordinary manager and the common experience of the philosopher are not merely a matter of what each one does or does not know, but also of what kind of person each one is. To dedicate the time, thought, and effort that it takes to become an expert in property management, one must endorse the values and objectives set by that art, much as a servant must make his own the values and goals of his master. This the philosopher refuses to do. He knows enough about property management to cater adequately to his needs and those of his friends. More than that would entail abandoning the values of Epicurean philosophy together with all hope of attaining serenity and happiness.

5. Philodemus on the Appropriate Sources of Income

Predictably, Philodemus's assessement of the traditional sources of income (XXII.6– XXIII.36) is also conducted according to criteria drawn from Epicurean ethics. The basis of his assessment consists in the kind of reasoning that Metrodorus uses against the Cynics. "His (sc. Metrodorus's) continuous effort has been to establish that occasional disturbances, cares, and labors are far more useful in the long run for the best way of life than the opposite choice" (XXII.9–18). Following him (cf. ἀκολουθοῦντες, XXII.17–18), Philodemus considers different ways of earning a living in the light of the hedonistic calculus and thus determines which ones are appropriate for the philosopher.

First, Philodemus refutes the traditional view that the best way of earning an income is to practice the military art—winning goods by the spear. In truth, only unwise and vainglorious men make that choice (XXII.17–28), presumably because they do not measure correctly the many pains of the military life against its few pleasures. So, Philodemus undertakes to refute those authors who praise the achievements of men of action and who consider philosophers inferior to such men.

> Indeed, they generally appear to attribute these [achievements] to the politicians and the men of action, so that one could often ask what in the world is left for those who [devote themselves to study] concerning the truth and who consider all these issues. For at least according to them, the people who do all the noble deeds that contribute to the tranquillity that derives from the most

important things (sc. politicians and military men) and those who contemplate the truth are not the same people, but obviously they will claim either that the ones who are wonderfully gifted regarding the search for truth [do not have] the excellence that achieves this aim (sc. tranquillity), or that nothing remarkable is accomplished because of it, [or that] if a city or army were led by those who excel in wisdom.... (XXII.28–48)

It is unclear which opponents Philodemus has in mind here. Whatever their identity may be, their accusations against the philosophers imply a complete dissociation of the practical from the contemplative life. They maintain that tranquillity "that is generated from the most important things" (XXII.39–40) results from the actions of politicians and military men, not from the theoretical contemplation of philosophers. "The most important things" are, presumably, things such as the independence of one's country, personal freedom, material prosperity, and so on.[35] The main assumption underlying the charge is that peace of mind crucially depends on external rather than internal, psychological factors. As Philodemus suggests, there are different ways in which the opponents can press their charge. One may contend that, although philosophers have intellectual virtues, they do not possess the kinds of virtues through which tranquillity is achieved, whereas men of action do. Alternatively, one may concede that tranquillity is the achievement of the philosopher but maintain that it has no value. Another suggestion could be that only some ideal ruler in the future, who would combine the virtues of the comtemplative and of practical men, would secure tranquillity for himself and the state (see XXII.46–XXIII.1). Philodemus reacts to these arguments by pointing to facts. The *Lives* of notorious men of action, such as Gellias of Sicily, Scopas of Thessaly, and the Athenians Kimon and Nicias,[36] reveal that they had neither practical nor contemplative wisdom; they were driven by vainglory and led miserable lives (XXII.20–28).

Philodemus evaluates other traditional sources of income on similar grounds.

---

35. Contrast the Epicurean meaning of τὰ κυριώτατα, namely, the fundamental principles of Epicurean philosophy (cf. *De elect.* IX.10; XI.8–9).

36. See notes 60 and 62.

It is [utterly] ridiculous to believe that it is good thing to earn an income from practicing the art of horsemanship. Earning an income "from the art of mining with slaves doing the labor" is unfortunate, and as to securing income "from both these sources by means of one's own labor," it is a mad thing to do. "Cultivating the land oneself in a manner involving work with one's own hands" is also wretched, while (cultivating it) "using other workers if one is a landowner" is appropriate for the good man. For it brings the least possible involvement with men from whom many disagreeable things follow, and a pleasant life, a leisurely retreat with one's friends, and a most dignified income to [those who are moderate]. Nor is it disgraceful to earn an income both from properties rented to tenants and from slaves who have skills or even arts that are in no way unseemly. (*De oec.* XXIII.1–22)

Philodemus does not seem to reject the equestrian art out of hand but simply points out that it is not a good thing, probably because it is strenuous and toilsome. But the possibility is left open, I think, that there might be circumstances in which the philosophically minded person might have to earn a living from engaging in that art. Provided that he does not hold false beliefs about its intrinsic worth, he may have to practice it to the extent that it is useful. Severe restrictions apply to making money from working in mines. It would be "crazy" for the philosopher to make a living by working himself at mining, and it would be "unfortunate" to do so by having his servants work at mining.[37] The former is rejected outright on account of the hedonistic calculus, whereas the latter is merely discouraged probably in the name of Epicurean philanthropy: Philodemus suggests that the philosopher should avoid making money in a manner that involves heavy toil and occasionally death for others, although he tacitly acknowledges, I think, that circumstances might sometimes necessitate such a distasteful course of action. He adopts a comparable attitude toward agriculture: working the land in person cannot be justified in hedonistic terms, but earning an income as a landowner through the agricultural labor of one's servants is highly recommended as "a most dignified' (εὐσχημονεστάτην, XXIII.17–18) source of income. The very occupation that the philosopher should not accept for himself, he should

---

37. See note 64.

tolerate and even desire for his farmers. Ultimately, the reason might be egoistic: the farmers' manual labor secures a pleasant life for the philosopher.[38] Two further sources of earning a living, which tradition considers ungentlemanly, are also legitimate on the grounds of the hedonistic calculus: rentals (probably of houses or other buildings, not of land); and the skillful work of slaves. In so far as neither of these sources involves excessive toil, and assuming that the slaves' occupations are not indecent,[39] the philosopher may get revenues from both (XXIII.18–22).

"However, these sources of income come second and third. The first and noblest thing is to receive back thankful gifts with all reverence in return for philosophical discourses shared with men capable of understanding them, as happened to Epicurus, and, [moreover], discourses that are truthful and free of strife and, [in short], serene, since in fact the acquisition of an income through [sophistical] and contentious speeches is [in no way] better than its acquisition through demagogical and slandering ones" (XXIII.22–36). There is a long tradition in Greek literature according to which the occupation of the philosopher is ranked first in order. However, the passage cited above contains the first instance in which the teaching of philosophy is identified as the first and best source of moneymaking: it perfectly suits the philosopher's lifestyle, and in addition it is not really payment, but gifts that the sage receives from thankful students in return for the privilege of conversing with him. This last point is brought out by the contrast between the sage's discourses and the speeches of sophists and demagogues (XXIII.32–36)—whom I take to be mainly teachers or practitioners of forensic or political rhetoric.[40] Unlike them, the sage does not sell his ideas, nor does he use them to get power. He imparts his wisdom in conversation and accepts tokens of gratitude from people who understand and appreciate him.[41] As to the landowner, we may think of him in terms of a gracious host who offers his country property as a peaceful retreat where philosophy flourishes and true enjoyment is attained.[42]

---

38. Again, see note 64.
39. As would be, for example, prostitution.
40. See note 56.
41. On the notion of gratitude and its role in contexts concerning payment for teaching, see Blank 1985.
42. See notes 65 and 66.

The Papyrus

PHerc. 1424 is one of the large collection of papyri excavated from the so-called Villa of the Papyri at Herculaneum in the mid-eighteenth century. These papyri, widely believed to have originated from Philodemus's own library, suffered carbonization during their long burial following the eruption of Vesuvius in 79 c.e. The majority of them were unrolled over the years with varying degrees of success and are still preserved at the Officina dei papiri ercolanesi, in the National Library in Naples. Despite their deteriorating condition, they can still be fruitfully read with the help of microscopes and the photographic technique known as multispectral imaging (MSI). In addition, we have the further evidence provided by pencil-drawn fascimiles (known as "apographs" or "disegni") that were produced by draughtsmen, mainly in the early nineteenth century. One set of these, the Oxonian apograph (O), is now in the Bodleian Library in Oxford, while another set, the Neapolitan apograph (N), is preserved in the Officina in Naples.[43]

The inventory of the Herculaneum papyri does not mention the name of the person or persons in the Officina who unrolled PHerc. 1424. It seems likely that the papyrus was unrolled in 1791 either by Gennaro Casanova or by Antonio Lentari or Gian Battista Malesci. The Neapolitan apograph (N) was probably drawn by Casanova in 1791–1792. In any case, N must have been drawn before the Oxonian apograph (O) prepared under the supervision of John Hayter sometime between 1802 and 1806. A second Neapolitan apograph was drawn by Carlo Orazi, probably in 1814. The autopsy of the papyrus and the use of multispectral images lend support to Jensen's claim (1906, x–xii) that N is far superior to both O and Orazi's Neapolitan apograph, which are in fact similar to each other: N has a fuller text than O; it contains in the margin *sovrapposti* and *sottoposti* (fragments of, respectively, later and earlier layers that need to be distinguished from the proper content of each column) lacking in O; where there are lacunae, the Neapolitan apographist indicates the size and number of the missing letters more accurately than the apographist who drew O; and many details indicate that the Neapolitan apographist was more careful and skilled than his counterpart. Consequently, Jensen's edi-

---

43. More information about the Herculaneum papyri can be found, for example, in Gigante 1995 and in the introduction to Sider 1997.

tion is primarily based on N, but also Jensen has marked the discrepencies that O exhibits where they seem to have some value in restoring the text. Information concerning the papyrus itself is found in Jensen's apparatus, and traces of letters found in N but omitted from the edition that Jensen used to establish his own text (Javarone 1827) are found both in Jensen's apparatus and in the *tabula* attached to his edition.

Physically, at the time of Jensen's edition, PHerc. 1424 was estimated to have had a length of approximately 2.20 meters and a width of approximately 20 centimeters. It was (and still is) glued on eight *cornici* (frames). The first frame contains fragments 1 and 2 and columns I, II; the second fragments A and B1, columns III–VI and fragment B2; the third columns VII–X; the fourth columns XI–XIV; the fifth columns XV–XVIII; the sixth columns XIX–XXII; the seventh columns XXIII–XXVI; and the eighth columns XXVII–XXVIII as well as the title of the work. The numbers of lines per column varies from forty-five to forty-nine, while the number of letters per line varies between eighteen and twenty-five. The top and bottom margins of the papyrus are very damaged or completely destroyed. While the first six first columns are extremely lacunose, the subsequent columns are well preserved and serve as the basis of an almost complete text to the end of the work. Five stichometric letters written in the left margin[44] indicate that the scroll initially contained approximately ninety-eight columns. Hence, following Jensen (1906, xvi), we may infer that the extant remains of PHerc. 1424 constitute approximately one quarter of the original papyrus scroll.

Palaeographically, PHerc. 1424 has been classified by Guglielmo Cavallo in Group P, together with other papyri of Philodemus's ensemble Περὶ κακιῶν (for instance, PHerc. 1008). The letters are even, regular, and clearly separated from one another. There are no abbreviations, ligatures, or, generally, cursive elements. Orthographically, the quality of the writing testifies to the scribe's ability and diligence. There are several idiosyncratic

---

44. Jensen (1906, xvi–xvii) indicates five places in which stichometric letters occur: a Π with a line over it, which is a *sovrapposto* in the margin of IV.38 but that belongs in fact to VI.38; an Υ in X.23; a Χ in XVIII.16; a Ψ in XXII.2; and a Ω with a line over it in XXV.42. As Jensen calculates, the successive stichometric letters of the alphabet occur 180 lines apart; assuming that the scroll begins with an A and ends with the Ω in XXV.42, the scroll probably contained approximately 4,500 lines distributed over approximately ninety-eight columns (for his justification of the numbers, see 1906, xvi–xvii).

elements[45] and also some mistakes that, however, are neatly corrected. When the scribe writes -ει instead of long -ι, he usually corrects the -ει by putting a dot over the -ι (see Jensen 1906, xi). When he makes a mistake of one letter, he usually writes the correction above the line.[46] On the other hand, when he makes a mistake in several successive letters, he corrects the mistaken letters by putting dots over them.[47] Concerning punctuation, the *paragraphos* is marked under the line of the left part of the column. There are three examples of a double *papagraphos* (XVIII.7; XXI.35; XXIV.19). The scribe almost never leaves a space at the end of a sentence. However, he quite frequently adds a point (marked with an asterisk by Jensen) at the end of a sentence, above the line. Besides, both at the end of the refutation of Philodemus's rivals (XII.2) and at the end of the book the scribe draws a *coronis*. Finally, at the left of some verses (frag. II.12; V.5; 13.7) there is a mark that looks like a line slanting upward to the right, but there is no firm indication as to what it may mean (see Jensen 1906, xii).

EDITIONS AND CONTRIBUTIONS TO THE TEXT

PHerc. 1424 was first edited by Thom Gaisford in *Herculanensium Voluminum pars I* (Gaisford 1824), 83–105, and soon afterward by Francesco Javarone in *Herculanensium voluminum quae supersunt tomus III* (Javarone 1827). Other editions previous to Jensen notably include: Karl Wilhelm Göttling, Ἀριστοτέλους Οἰκονομικός. Ἀνωνύμου Οἰκονομικά. Φιλοδήμου Περὶ κακιῶν καὶ τῶν ἀντικειμένων ἀρετῶν θ' (Göttling 1830); Georg Friedrich Schömann, *Specimen observationum in Theophrasti Oeconomicum et Philodemi librum IX de virtutibus et vitiis* (Schömann 1839); Johann Adam Hartung, *Philodems Abhandlungen über die Haushaltung und über den Hochmut und Theophrasts Haushaltung und Charakterbilder, griechisch und deutsch, mit kritischen und erklärenden Anmerkungen* (Hartung 1857); the contributions of Leonhard Spengel in the serial *Gelehrte Anzeigen* (Munich) 7 (1838): 1001–16; 9 (1839): 505–28, 533–36; and Heinrich Perron's Ph.D. dissertation, "Textkritische Bemerkungen zu Philodems Oeconomicus" (1895).

---

45. See Jensen's index verborum.
46. Jensen notes the two exceptions to that practice: in VII.3 the -α has changed into an -ε, and in XV.9 the -κ has changed into a -χ.
47. A good example is XI.32.

In the present volume, the text of PHerc. 1424 is based primarily on Jensen's text, but it also contains new readings. I have worked from my own readings of the papyrus in 1989–1990 and in 1995, from the originals as well as copies of N and O, and from the multispectral images of the papyrus (MSI). Textual footnotes are intended to serve as a very limited apparatus, indicating the new readings and juxtaposing them with Jensen's text. In some cases a brief explanation or comment is supplied as well. The translation uses square brackets to indicate those places in which a given passage or word is heavily restored, whereas it does not use square brackets for supplementations that appear to me fairly certain. Parentheses are intended to clarify or to complete the meaning of a word or phrase, but neither the parentheses nor what is included in them correspond to anything in the Greek text. Philodemus's parenthetical phrases are placed in between dashes. The text offered in this volume differs in several places from Jensen's text regarding punctuation, in part because of new conjectures indicated in the apparatus and in part because the new punctuation reflects a different sense of the flow, musicality, or structure of the relevant passages of the Greek text. The introduction offers an overview and analysis of the central argument of the text as well as information concerning the papyrus. The Notes section following the text and translation supplies additional comments about textual matters, explains particularly obscure passages and arguments, contains relevant historical or factual information, and points to conceptual and philosophical connections between different parts of the text and also between *On Property Management* and other works by Philodemus and other Epicureans. Importantly, several of these notes highlight Philodemus's intertextuality, the way he reads and engages with the "economic" works of his main rivals, Xenophon and Theophrastus. For *On Property Management* offers a unique opportunity to see Philodemus at work as an interpreter and a critic of treatises that have the same subject as his own book but that reflect different philosophical perspectives.

The present volume aims to be accessible to readers who have an interest in the subject but do not necessarily know Greek. The text and the translation are juxtaposed on left and right pages, respectively, and one can read the one without looking at the other. Although Greek terms are occasionally used in the introduction and the Notes, nonetheless they also are always translated. There is much material for specialists as well—classicists, philosophers, and historians particularly interested in ancient conceptions of οἰκονομία, property management, and their admittedly tenuous relation to modern economics. The subtlety, complexity, and importance of Philodemus's treatment of that topic and also the new readings of the papyrus ought to point to the need for a new critical edition of PHerc. 1424.

TEXT AND TRANSLATION

Φιλοδήμου περὶ κακιῶν καὶ τῶν ἀντικειμένων ἀρετῶν
καὶ τῶν ἐν οἷς εἰσι καὶ περὶ ἅ θ (= περὶ οἰκονομίας)

ColumN A

········· ἔτι δὲ καὶ κοσ]μ[η-
τικὸν εἶναι καὶ χρη]στ[ι]κὸ[ν
················ κ]α[ὶ ὑ]π[αρ-
χόντων· τούτων γὰρ] ἕνεκα   5
κἀκείνων δεόμεθα]. διε[ιρῆ-
σθαι δὲ δεῖ ἕκαστον], καὶ πλεί[ω
τὰ κάρπιμα τῶν ἀ]κάρπων ε[ἶ-
ναι, καὶ τὰς ἐργασί]ας οὕτω ν[ε-
νεμῆσθαι δεῖ, ὅπ]ως μὴ ἅμα [κιν-   10
δυνεύηι πᾶσιν. πρ]ὸς δὲ φυλ[α-
κὴν τοῖς Π]ερσικοῖ[ς] συμφέ[ρει
χρῆσθαι] καὶ τοῖς Λακωνικο[ῖς. καὶ
ἡ Ἀττικὴ δ]ὲ οἰκονομία χρήσιμος (ἀπ]οδιδόμενοι γὰρ ὠ-   15
νοῦνται) καὶ ἡ] τοῦ τα[μ]είου [θέ-
σις ἐν ταῖς μ]ικροτέραι[ς] οἰ[κονο-
μίαις. Περσ]ικά τ᾽ [ἦν τὸ] πά[ντα
τετάχθαι κ]αὶ ·····χας
················ ναπι   20
········· Δί]ων· οὐδεὶς [γὰρ
ἐπιμελεῖται ὁ]μοίως [τῶν] ἀ[λ-
λοτρίων καὶ] τῶ[ν] οἰκείων, [ὥσ-
τε ὅσα ἐνδέχ]ε[τα]ι δι᾽ αὐτο[ῦ
ποιεῖσθαι χρὴ τ]ὴν ἐ[πι]μέλ[ει-   25
αν. καὶ τὸ τοῦ Πέ]ρσ[ου καὶ τὸ
τοῦ Λίβυος] ··· μη ······

PHILODEMUS, ON VICES AND THE OPPOSITE VIRTUES AND THE PEOPLE IN WHOM THEY OCCUR AND THE SITUATIONS IN WHICH THEY ARE FOUND, BOOK 9 (= ON PROPERTY MANAGEMENT*)

ON PROPERTY MANAGEMENT

COLUMN A

[… and in addition, he is skilled in the arrangement and in the use … and of possessions. For it is] for the sake of [these things that we need those things as well.[1] Moreover, [each must be distinguished, and "fruitful" possessions must be more than] "unfruitful" ones, [and the tasks must have been distributed] so as [not to endanger them all at once.] Regarding the preservation (sc. of property), it is profitable to use the Persian and the Spartan methods.[2] [As to the Attic method] of property management,[3] it is useful as well (for the Athenians [purchase] at the same time as they sell), and [the office] of the treasurer [does not exist in] the less-significant estates. [The Persian method consisted in having all the possessions] arranged in order and[4] … [Dion].[5] For nobody [takes care of the goods of others and of his own goods] in the same way, [and therefore one should manage one's own property] by oneself, [as much as this is possible. The … of the Persian and of the Libyan …]

COLUMN B

πρὸς οἰκ]ο[ν]ομία[ν], ἐ[γ]ε[ίρε-
σθαι χρὴ πρ]ότερο[ν] δε[σπότας
οἰκετῶν] καὶ καθ[εύδ]ει[ν ὕ-
στερον, καὶ] μηδέποτ[ε ὅλην
οἰκίαν ἀφύ]λακτον ε[ἶναι, ὥσ-   5
περ πόλιν], μήτε νυκτὸς [μή-
τε ἡμέρας, ε]ἰωθέναι τε δι[ανί-
στασθαι ν]ύκτωρ· τοῦτο [γὰρ
καὶ πρὸς ὑ]γίειαν καὶ οἰκον[ο-
μ]ία[ν καὶ] φιλοσοφίαν χρή[σ]ι-   10
μον· [καὶ] ἐν ταῖ[ς] μικραῖς κτ[ή-
σεσι[ν ὁ Ἀττι]κὸς [τρό]πος τῆς
διαθ[έσεως τῶν ἐ]π[ικα]ρπι-
ῶν χρ[ήσιμος, ἐν δ]ὲ ταῖς με-
γά[λαις διαμερισθέντ]ων [καὶ   15
τῶν [πρὸς ἐνιαυτὸν κα]ὶ τῶ[ν
κα[τὰ μῆνα δαπαν]ω[μέ]νω[ν,
ὁμοίως δὲ καὶ περὶ] σ[κευῶν

COLUMN I

[··· Εἰ μὲν ··· ὑπελάμβανεν
ὅτι τῆς συν[ήθως νοουμένης
οἰκον[ομ]ίας οὐ[κ ἔ]σ[τι]ν ἔργο[ν   5
τὸ [ε]ὖ οἰκεῖν τὸ[ν] ἴδιον οἶκον
καὶ τὸ ποιεῖν τὸν ἀλλότριον
εὖ οἰκεῖσθαι, λαμβανομένου
τοῦ ε[ὖ] τοῦ μεγαλωστὶ συμ-
φέροντος καὶ μακαρίως, ἀλ-   10
λὰ τὸ πορίζειν πολλὰ χρή-
ματα καὶ φυλάττειν πῶς δι-
αμενεῖ τὰ πορισθέντα καὶ
προϋπάρχοντα καὶ κατὰ τοῦ-
το τὸ εὖ [ο]ἰκεῖν τὸν ἴδιον οἶ-   15
κον καὶ π[οι]εῖν οἰκεῖσθαι τὸν
ἀλλότριον, εἴ γε σύνηθες ἦν
τιθέναι [τ]ότε ἢ καὶ νῦν ἐσ-

COLUMN B

[... in matters of property management the masters should wake up before the servants and should go to sleep after them; and the house should] never [be left completely] unguarded, [just as a city should not] either during the night [or during the day], and it should be customary [to rise] during the night.[6] [For] this is useful for health as well as for property management and for philosophy.[7] [Further, the Attic manner of the disposition of revenues is useful] in the small estates, [whereas, in the large estates, once both the annual revenues and the monthly expenses have been distributed, [these matters should be handed over to the overseers]; and the same holds regarding the household equipment][8]

COLUMN I

[... if he (sc. Xenophon) ... supposed that] the function of property management, [as it is ordinarily understood, is] not to govern one's own home well and to make other people's homes be governed well, with ["well"] taken to mean beneficially on a large and prosperous scale,[9] but rather to gain many riches[10] and to take care as to how the riches that have been gained and those that belonged to one beforehand will be preserved, and that it is precisely in this respect that (the function of household management is) to govern one's own home well and to make other people's homes be well governed—if, at any rate, it was customary to apply this (term) in those days (viz. Xenophon's) in the way that it is now, no one would resent

τιν, οὐκ ἂν φθονῆσαι τις, εἰ δὲ
κατὰ τοῦ προλε[χ]θέν[τ]ος, οὐ-   20
κ ἂν συ[γ]χωρ[ήσειεν ·······

Fragment I

·ηι καὶ το ·············
σ·· αι το ·············
·ος ··· ισλ ·············
χρήμ]ατα καὶ ἐπ ········
χρήμ]ατα μ[ισ]θο ········   5
····ε μι[σθ]ὸν σ······ [τε-
λεῖν] τε ὄ[σα δ]εῖ καὶ [περιο]υσί-
αν π]οιῶν αὔξειν τ[ὸ]ν ο[ἶκ]ον
····ε μηδ᾽ ἐφεστη[κ]ὼς αὐ-
[τός]¹ γ]ίνεσθαι τὴν ἀ[πο]φορ[ὰ]ν   10
···· π]αραγγελλόμ[ενο]ν
···· μη ταῖς παρακ[ειμέν]αις²
ἐπιστ]ήμαις ἡ οἰκονο[μία
παρα]πλησία καθε·······
··· εαυτηνενοε³·······   15
···· μὴ μόνον ἡ οἰκ[ία, ἀλλ]ὰ
καὶ ὅσ]α τις ἔξω κέκτηται, κυ-
ρίω]ς ὑπακουομένου τοῦ
κε]κτῆσθαι. τὸ δ᾽ ἐχ[θ]ρ[οὺς
κεκ]τῆσθαί τ[ι]νας ο[ὐ λέγε-   20
ται κυ]ρίως, ὃν τρόπ[ον ····
···· σκηματα τὸ ·······
·· υ · σ μαμενοι ········
····· ιζοντας ··········
···· α · καὶ βλά[β ········   25
παρασκε]υάζομεν ·······
········ ασκο ········
········ η μεγ ······

---

1. Sedley, Tsouna; αὐ-|··· Jensen.
2. Tsouna; παρακο···ιαις Jensen.
3. Tsouna; εαυτην ἐνοε Jensen.

it. But if, on the other hand, (it was customary to apply it to) what we mentioned earlier, one would not [concede] …

FRAGMENT I

[… wages … and to accomplish all that is necessary] and to increase [his estate by making a profit … nor having himself supervised … the payment to be made … giving orders] … property management (is) resembling [the disciplines closely connected (to it)] … not only [the house, but also what] one possesses outside the house, if "to possess" is understood in [the principal sense of the term]. On the other hand, the phrase ["certain people possess enemies" is not said in the principal sense, in a manner that …][11]

FRAGMENT II

···ιαιε···········
··ν κακῆς··········   5
πό]νωι πόν············
ἐκεῖνον ἐν·············
πιστα············[πολ-
λὰ δὴ κτή[ματα··········
τὰ παραπλ[ήσια········   10
γῆ κτῆμα μ············
παντὸς ἀπ············
γοι δ᾽ ὁ τοσα[ῦτα········
κατὰ τρόπον··········
πρὸς πορισμ[ὸν········   15
καὶ χρῆται··········

COLUMN IIIA

··············· ν·····
············ δηλε. ω. ε
·········· ἐ]πιστήμονος
······ κα]ὶ μάλιστα πάντων
······· τὰς ὠφελίας αὐτῶι   5
παρασκε]υάζουσιν· ὥστε κἂν
τὸν ἀγαθ]ὸν οἰκονόμον λέ-
γωμεν τὸ]ν κτημάτων καὶ
χρημάτων π]ο[ρισ]τήν, περι-
γενή]σ[εσθ]αι καὶ ταύτας ἐν   10
τοῖ]ς κτήμ[ασιν] καὶ χρήμασιν
ἃ δι]οικονομεῖ, καὶ ὑπάρχειν
ἔρ]γον αὐτ[ο]ῦ τὸ μακα[ρί]ω[ς
οἶ]κον οἰκεῖν καὶ διδάσκειν [ἄλ-
λο]ν τερπνότερα πράγματα,   15
οἶ]α ζητῶν οὐκ ἄν τις εὕρο[ι]⁴
ἄλλ]ος ἐπιθαυμάζων ἄν, ···
··· ος ὁ τοιοῦτος λέγει ···

_____

4. Sedley; εὕρε[ν Jensen.

Fragment II

[... of a bad ... through labor ... many fields ... the things resembling ... the land ... field ... of all ... the person who ... so many things ... according to the manner (of) ... for gain ... and he uses ...][12]

Column IIIa

... of a person who has expert knowledge ... and most of all ... (those things that) [procure] benefits for himself. So, even if we say that the [good] property manager is a [provider] of possessions and money, these (benefits) too will [abound] in the possessions and money that he manages, and his job is to govern the house prosperously and teach [another person] more pleasant things, such as [another person] would not have discovered if he looked for them, although he admired them ... This kind

ἄλ]λου ποεῖν οἶκον οἰκ[εῖσθαι
[κα]λῶς⁵ ἂν αὐ[τ]ὸς ν ·· χι ···   20
···· οὐκ ἔχ[ειν] ·········
··· νται φιλ ···········
··· ωντηλησλ ······ ειτα
···· λιστα χρωμ ·······
······ ις καλῶς ·······   25
····· ν ἄλλων γρά[φομ]εν
ἀ]γαθοῦ οἰκον[όμου ···]μν·
ὥ]στε ὠφελεῖ[σθαι ····]υ ··
·· κέτι ············ των
·· ν σοφι ·· εχ ······ ν ··   30
· ινιοντος · λλ ······ γων
αι ······· αρι ····· περι ·

Column IV

ως οὐδέποτε τῆς συνηθεία[ς
κ]αλούσης, ἐξ ὧν παρακόψας
ο]ὗτος αὐτὴν πειρᾶται συλλο-
γ]ίζεσθαι, καὶ δεσπότας ἔχειν
βιάζετ]α[ι] τὰς κωλυούσας κα-   5
κίας] καὶ πονηροτάτους, ἀργί-
α[ν ψ]υχῆς καὶ ἀμελίαν καὶ κυβε[ία]ν καὶ κακομειλί[α]ν, καὶ
τ[οὺς] ἐργαζομένους [κ]αὶ μη-
χ[α]νωμένους προ[σόδους,   10
κ[ατατ]ρίβ[ο]ντας δὲ τ[οὺς οἴ-
κ[ους π]ο[ιεῖ] δεσποτῶν [πάνυ <δούλους>⁶
[κακῶν]⁷, λ[ι]χν[ε]ίας καὶ οἰνο-
φλυγ]ίας καὶ φιλοτ[ι]μίας, οἷς
δ[εῖ] μάχεσθαι μᾶλλ[ον ἢ π]ο-   15
λε]μ[ίοι]ς ··· μεντ ······

of man says ... [to achieve the good administration of someone else's] house [he himself would ... well ... of others ... we write that ... of the good property manager ... so as to benefit ...][13]

Column IV

... [although] ordinary language never uses [these names in this] way, this man crazily tries to deduce it from these names and [forces] it to have as masters, and as extremely wicked ones at that, the vices that act as hindrances,[14] that is, idleness of the soul, carelessness, gambling, and inappropriate conversation, and turns those people who work and make [profits] for themselves but who [squander their household goods] into the [slaves of bad] masters—gluttony and drunkenness and ambition[15]— things against which one must fight more than against [enemies] ... of

·· νῦν ἐκείνων κ ·······
··· αι · σ ···· ινακ ·······
············ ι ········
············ λι ······   20
··········· οει ········
········ αρ ······ ρι ····
κακίαι δέσπ]οιναι τομ ·····
···· κα]ὶ πο[λεμί]ων μᾶλ[λον
········ α · ν τοίνυν οτ ···   25
······· προσδεῖ]σθαι χρη[μά-
των] ······ δσ ···· [π]έντε [μνᾶς
········ προσδεῖσθαι λ ···
··· πέ]νη[τ]ας εἶναι τοὺς ἑκα-
τονταπλ]άσια; π[ῶς δὲ] τοῖς μὲ[ν   30
ἱκανὰ ἔσε]σθαι, τοῖς δὲ μή;
καὶ πῶς τ]ῆι συνηθείαι τὸν
μὲν αὐτῶν] δεῖ [πτ]ωχὸν κα-
λεῖν, τὸν] δὲ πλούσιον; κα[ὶ
········ ρι · σιν τὸν μὲν   35
······ τὸ]ν δὲ γω · α[σ ·· ε]ιν
········ ετι ·· μεν ·····
·········· ν ··· ασμ · ε ···
········ α · ν · ασεφαλοι ··

Column V

··· προσα]γορε[ύ]ειν, τὸν δὲ μ[ε-
τ᾽ ἐμφάσεω]ς καὶ πτωχόν, ἀλλὰ
δ]οξαστικῶς, οὐ προληπτικῶς
κατὰ συνήθειαν. Τὸ μὲν οὖν
οὐ πραγματικὸν ἀεὶ Σωκρά-   5
της εἶχε, [τ]ὸ δ᾽ ἱκανὸν αὐτῶι
πέντε μνᾶς εἶναι πρὸς τά-
ναγκαῖα [κ]αὶ τὰ φυσικὰ τῶν
ἀνθρώπων ἐπιζητήματα [καὶ
κεν[ὴν εἶν]αι τὴν ἐν τῶι ζῆν   10
εὐετηρίαν καὶ μηδὲν προσ-
δ]εῖσθαι τῶν πλειόν[ω]ν ἐπ᾽αὐ-
τήν, ἄπορον τῷ ἔργῳ καὶ τῷ

those … of enemies more … therefore … to need money in addition …
five minae … to need in addition … [How is it possible] for people who
have a hundred times more to be poor? [How could it be] that some will
have [enough] to live on, whereas others will not? [And how] could we, in
accordance with ordinary usage, call the one [of them] poor but the other
rich? And … the one … the other …

COLUMN V

… (it is his practice) [to call] (the one person rich) and the other, emphatically, poor, but (he speaks in that manner) as a matter of opinion, not
preconception in accordance with ordinary usage. Surely, Socrates always
had the characteristic of impracticality. Besides, as regards his claim that
five minae seem to him sufficient for the necessary and natural needs of
men,[16] that prosperity in life [is something empty], and that he does not
need anything more in addition to those, it is impracticable and conflicts
with reason. But indeed also, judging from the written record of what has

νῷ μαχόμενον.⁸ Ἀλλὰ δὴ καὶ
τ]οῖς ὑπ' Ἰσχομάχου λελέχθαι   15
καὶ ὑπὸ Σ[ωκρ]άτους προσωμο-
λ]ογ[ῆσθαι γ]εγραμμένοις παρὰ τὴν οἰκο]νομίαν κα[ὶ] τὴ[ν
καλοκάγαθία]ν ἐμάνθανον
·········· σ οὐδ' ἦσαν ἀσ-   20
··········θον, τὸ δ' ἀ-
·········· ἔ]χειν καὶ ἀ-
··············· στον
··············· καὶ πα-
······ ἐ]μφαίνει δ' οὖν   25
······τεσι··ος οὐδ' οἱ
······ειλ··οι πέντε
·α·····\·····δ·· κως ἱκα[νὰ
και·····\····· δὲ τοσαῦτα
βεβα·····\··· Κρ[ιτ]όβουλος   30
··θης············\······ερ··
··πλ············\···········
······δ············\··· της πολ-
—ς τυχούσ[ης·\····ασ ἡ κτῆ-
—νοκτοτου·····\··ξε······   35
—ἔ]πιπλα πο·····\·········
—ἔχοντας λ·····\···········
—χ]ρῆσθαι μ ·····\··········
—εσ]τιν χρ·····\···········
——ασε·········\·······   40

Column VI

···········την ὡς οὐ-
κ ἄξι]ο[ν ἀνδρὸς σώ]φρονος [οἷ-
ος Ἰ[σ]χόμαχος ἦν, ὃν θρ[α]συ[νό-
μενος οὐ μόνον οἰκονομι-
κὸν ἀλλὰ καὶ καλὸν κἀγαθὸ[ν   5

---

8. 12–13: Perron; ἐπ' αὐ-|ταῖς] ὅρον [θέμενον], καὶ τ[ῶι | ν]ῶι μαχ[όμ]ενον
Jensen.

been said by Ischomachus and [agreed on] by Socrates, [in addition to property management] they were learning [moral excellence][17] ... nor were they ... but indicates ... nor the ... five ... [sufficient] ... so many ... Critoboulos ... [the possession] ...

Left Part of the Column
[... who happened to be ... furniture ... to use ...]

Column VI

... [for it is something unworthy of a prudent man], [such as] Ischomachus was, whom Xenophon [rashly] introduced not only as a man practiced in property management, but also as a person of moral excellence and as the teacher of Socrates in both respects.[18] Well, concerning

Ξενοφῶν εἰσῆγεν καὶ Σωκ[ρά-
τους ἀμφοτέρω[ς] διδάσκ[α-
λον. Ἀλλ᾽ ὑπὲρ μὲν τῶν Ἰσ[χο-
μάχου μετὰ ταῦτ[α θ]εω[ρήσο-
μεν, τοῖς δ᾽ ἐπεσκ[ε]μμέ[νοις,   10
ἐν ο]ῖς ὁ Σωκράτ[ης αὐτὸς τὸν
Κριτόβουλον [προσποιεῖται
διδάξαι τὴν οἰκο[ν]ο[μικὴν ἐ-
πιστήμην ὡς μαθησ[όμενον
διὰ μιᾶς ἀκροάσε[ως τὴν τη-   15
λικαύτην, ἑρμην[είας ἀδιαλη-
ψίαι τὴν αὐτὴν οὐκ ἔο[ικε θεῖ-
ναι πώποτε· φ[ήσ]ας [δ᾽] ο[ἰ]κο[νο-
μήσειν ὁ μηθ[αμόθ]εν μ[αν-
θά]νειν ἐν[δεδωκὼς καὶ ἐπι-   20
δ]είξειν δ············
····· κ ···············
·· εαι μ·············   25
καθ᾽ ὃν δ[ήποτε ··········
··οθει. ············
ἀλλ᾽ εἰκότως ··········
οἱ μὲν ἄπορο[ι ὄντες ·····
······τοὺς [μεν······   30
···· τοὺς δε ···········
δὲ τοῦτο πά[σχειν ········
τω υπερασο ············
δ᾽ [ο]ὐδὲν τ·············
με ···············   35

Column II

[Παντὶ γάρ, εἰ καὶ μὴ βαθυτέρα τις ὑ-   0
πείη θε[ωρία, καὶ ἵππων πρόχει-
ρον μανθάνειν καὶ [ἀνθρώπων
τὰς ἡλικίας. Ἀλλὰ μὴν καὶ τὸ γα-
μετὰς γυναῖκας ἐνίους ἔχειν
συνέργως εἰς χρηματισμόν,   5
τοὺς δὲ πάνυ βλαπτικῶς, οὐ-
κ ἠγνόει Κριτόβουλος ἐν μέ-

the positions of Ischomachus, [we shall examine them] later. On the other hand, regarding the passages that have already been examined, in which Socrates [himself affects] to teach Critoboulos the discipline of property management as if [he were going to learn] such a vast discipline from a single lecture, they never yet [seem to assume] the same meaning, because of [failure] to distinguish between different meanings.[19] [And the man who has conceded that he does not learn from any source, by affirming that he will discuss the subject of property management and will show that][20] ... ... but reasonably ... on the one hand, some people [who are] without resources ... some ... while others ... [suffer] this ...[21]

COLUMN II

[... It is easy for everyone] to learn the age [of horses and men,* even if no deeper underlying theory is available]. Indeed, Critoboulos was aware of the fact, which is common knowledge, that some men have wives who act in a cooperative manner with the goal of increasing the property, whereas

---

* I leave untranslated Jensen's lines 0–1 because they do not have any basis in Xenophon's text.

σωι κείμενον. Εἰ δ᾽ ἀναγκαῖόν
ἐστι γαμετὴ καὶ λυσιτελὲς
εἰς τὴν φιλόσοφον οἰκονομί- 10
αν καὶ καθόλου τὸν εἰρηναῖ-
ον βίον, ἔτι δὲ εἰ πᾶσα δυνατὴ
γυνὴ τὰ προσήκοντα διδά-
σκεσθαι καὶ πάντων δεῖ τῶν
ἀμ[α]ρτανομένων τὸν ἄνδρα 15
τὴν αἰτίαν ἔχ[ε]ιν ἢ τινῶν, οὐ-
κ ἴσως ᾔδει, καὶ π[αρ]ὰ [Σωκ]ράτους
ὀρθῶς ἂν ἠξίο[υ μ]α[ν]θάνειν,
ὁ δ᾽ Ἀσπασίαν αὐτῶι συνιστάν[ει]⁹
ὡς ἐπισ]τημονέστερον αὐτ[οῦ 20
πάντ᾽ ἐ]πιδείξουσα[ν]· ὃ δ᾽ αὐτ[ὸς
ἐν τῆι ὑ]φ[ηγήσε]ι νομίζει [γυ-
ναῖκα κ]οινω[νὸ]ν ἀγα[θὴν οὖ-
σαν οἴκ]ου πάν[υ] ἀντ[ίρροπον
ἐπὶ τἀγ]αθὸν εἶν[αι τἀνδρί, 25
καὶ ὡς ἔρχ]εται μὲ[ν εἰς τὴν
οἰκίαν ὡ]ς ἐπὶ τὸ πο[λὺ τ]ὰ κτήματα δι]ὰ τῶν τἀ[ν]δρὸς πρά-
ξεων, δ]απανᾶται δὲ [τὰ] πλεῖστα διὰ] τῶν τῆς γυναικ[ὸς 30
ταμιε]υμάτων, κ[αὶ εὖ μ]ὲ[ν τούτων γι]νομένων [αὔ]ξ[ον]τ[αι οἱ
οἶκ]οι, κακῶς δ[ὲ μ]ειοῦνται,
[ἤδη]¹⁰ ψεῦδός ἐστι· εἰ δὲ μή γε,
εὔηθ]ες· εἰ δὲ μή γ[ε], ἄδηλο[ν, τί- 35
νος ἤθ]ελε[ν] ἔνε[κ]α κέρδο[υς ⋯
⋯νος·πο⋯⋯⋯⋯⋯
⋯ οἱ σώφρον[ες ⋯⋯⋯⋯
⋯⋯αιρ⋯⋯⋯⋯⋯
⋯ ο]ὔτε τ⋯⋯⋯⋯ 40
⋯⋯αι·τα·αλλαι·εγ⋯⋯
⋯⋯⋯⋯ ἐργατη⋯⋯
⋯⋯⋯⋯·ταи⋯⋯

---

9. Sedley; συνιστάν[ειν] Jensen.
10. Perron; [κα]ὶ Jensen.

others have wives who act in a very damaging way. However, whether a wife is something necessary as well as useful to the management of the household in a philosophical manner and, generally, to the peaceful life, and moreover whether every woman is able to learn her duties, and whether the husband must bear the responsibility of all (her) mistakes or some of them, all these things perhaps Critoboulos did not know and he could be right to endeavor to learn them from Socrates, yet Socrates recommends Aspasia to him on the ground that she will show him [everything] in a more expert manner than he himself would. As regards the beliefs that he [himself] puts forward [in his exposition], [namely, that when the woman does her own share of work in the household she is just as important in every respect as the man with regard to the achievement of the good, and that material possessions come into the house mostly through] the activities of the man, [whereas most of them] are consumed through the stewardship of the woman, [and that if these things are done well then the estates increase], whereas if they are done badly they decrease, [this much] is false. And if they are not false, they are at least [naïve].[22] Or if not that, it still remains unclear [for the sake of what gain one would be willing to … the prudent men … nor …]

COLUMN VII

ἄλλων ὄφελος οὐκ εἶναι [τι-
θέναι μώρου νομίζω· ζητ[ῶ
δ']¹¹ ὄντινα τὰ ῥηθέντ' ἐπαίδευ-
εν, εἰ μὴ τὸν ταῦτ' ἐπεγνωκό-
τα. Καὶ μὴν ἅ γε λέγει περὶ τοῦ   5
ἄρχειν καὶ παιδεύε[ιν] τὰ διδα-
σκόμενα ζῷα παρατιθεὶς μα-
κρά τ' ἐστιν καὶ ὑπὸ τῶν γεωρ-
γούντων θεωρούμενα καὶ
ἐπιτηδευόμενα· π[ρὸς τῷ]¹² ἀνε-   10
κτά, φαίνεσθα[ι] καὶ ὑπὸ φιλο-
σόφου κελευόμενα ποιεῖν
τὸν ἐπίτροπον καὶ ὑπ' αὐτοῦ
συντελούμενα. Τὰ παραπλή-
σια δ' ἐμοὶ δοκεῖ καὶ περὶ τοῦ   15
διδάσκειν ἀπέχεσθαι τῶν
δεσποσύνων καὶ μὴ κλέπτειν,
εἰ καὶ τραγῳδεῖται, μετάγειν
λέγοντος ἔκ [τε] τῶν νομι-
κῶν Δράκοντος καὶ Σόλω-   20
νος καὶ τῶν βασιλικῶν· εἰ δ[ὲ]
κα[ὶ] δικαίους δυνατὸν εἶνα[ι
ποιεῖν [ἠξί]ου τὸν ἐπίτρο-
πο]ν διδάσκειν, τοῖς [καθ'] ὕπνον
αὐτ]ὸν ἡγοῦμαι δο[ξαζ]ομέ-   25
ν]οις ὅμοια λέγειν. Ἀλλὰ γὰρ
ο]ὐδὲν ἔτι δεῖ προσδιατρίβειν
τ]οῖς Ξεν[ο]φῶντος οἰκονο-
μ]ικοῖς, τῶν ἐφεξῆς γεωργι-
κὴν] τέχνην περιεχόντων,   30
ἣν] ἀπ' ἰδίας ἐμπειρίας, οὐκ ἀπὸ
φι]λοσ[ο]φίας γίνεσθαι συμβαί-

---

11. Jensen's conjecture ζητ[ῶ | δ'] in VII.2–3 is eminently plausible in
the light of the parallel with XI.38–39.
    12. Sedley; π[ῶς δ'] Jensen.

Column VII

...[23] to posit that (beyond what he himself knows, his bailiff) has no need of anything else, I consider the mark of a fool.[24] And I wonder who has been educated by the doctrines mentioned above, other than the person who has already approved of them. Then, what he says about the roles of the master and of the instructor citing as evidence examples of trained animals is lengthy and is understood as well as put into practice by the farmers, [quite apart from the fact that] these things appear acceptable both when issued as orders by the philosopher for the bailiff to carry out and when (simply) carried out by him. Similar remarks seem to me to hold also with regard to teaching (the servants) to keep their hands off the master's property and not to steal, even if he exaggerates in a manner befitting tragedy when he speaks of deriving these principles from the laws of both Dracon and Solon and from royal decrees. But if, further, he thought it possible to teach the property manager the capacity of making people just, then I consider him to be saying things similar to [the beliefs that we entertain in] our dreams. But there is no need to spend any more time on Xenophon's treatise on property management, since its next subject is the art of farming, which as a matter of fact derives from personal experience, not from philosophy.[25] Besides, (this art) [by its nature] is neither a neces-

νε]ι· πρ[ο]σέτι δ' οὔτ' ἀναγ[κ]αία γι-
νώ]σκ[ε]σθαι τοῖς φιλοσόφοις
πέφυκεν] οὔτ' οἰκεῖα τὰ κατ' αὐ-   35
τὴν ἔργα] συντελεῖσθαι δι' αὐ-
τῶν. Δ]ῆλον δή, διότι καὶ πρὸς
τὰ] π[λεῖ]στα τῶν Θεοφράστου
διειλέ]γμεθα ταῖς δυνάμε-
σιν] ἐκεῖθεν κεκεφαλαι[ω]μέ-   40
να, μ]ᾶλλον δὲ καὶ τὰ τῶν ἄλ-
λων·] ἅπαντες γὰρ ὡς ὑπερ[έ-
χον] μετηλλεύκασιν, ὅ ποτε
καὶ] Θεόφραστος· ἀποψόμε-
θα δ' ἐ]ν οἷς διαλλάττει. Περίερ-   45
γα τ]οίνυν [ἃ] προέθηκ[ε]ν· οὐ-
δὲ]ν γὰρ εἰς οἰκονομικὴν

COLUMN VIII

τὸ διαφέρειν τῆς πο[λιτικῆς,
κᾶν εἰ ψεῦδός ἐστιν τὸ τὴν πο-
λιτικὴν πάντως μὴ μοναρ-
χίαν εἶναι καὶ τὸ τὴν οἰκονο-
μικὴν πάντως μοναρχίαν   5
κ]αὶ μήποτε ἀναλογοῦντ' εἶ-
ν]αι περὶ ἑκατέραν· οὐδὲ τὸ τῶν
τ]εχνῶν τινὰς μὲν οἷς χρῶν-
ται ποιεῖν, τινὰς δὲ καὶ μή·* βλε-
πόμενον δ' ἄλλως πᾶσιν, ὅτι   10
τῶν εἰρημένων ἐστὶ συστή-
σασθαί τε καὶ χρῆσθαι· καὶ τὸ
τί πόλις ἐστὶν ἀποδιδόναι
κ]αὶ ταῦτ' ἐναργέστατον ὑ-
πάρχον· καὶ τὸ πρότερον οἰ-   15
κίαν πόλεως συστῆναι, διὸ
κα]ὶ τὴν οἰκονομικὴν τῆς πο-
λ]ιτικῆς. Τῶν δ' ὑπὲρ τῆς οἰκονομι-
κῆ]ς ἴδιον τὸ μέρη λέγειν τῆς
οἰ[κ]ίας ἄνθρωπον καὶ κτῆ-   20
σιν, ἴδι[ο]ν δ[ὲ κ]αὶ τὸ τὴν ἑκά-

sary object of the philosophers' [knowledge], nor are [the tasks pertaining to it] suited to being carried out [through their advice].[26] Indeed, it is clear that we have also, in effect, argued against Theophrastus's chief views and those of others.[27] For everybody has mined what Theophrastus too once mined, as being of superior value. However, we shall see in what respects he differs (from Xenophon). Well, then, [the things] he says in the way of an introduction[28] are superfluous. For it is irrelevant to the discipline of property management

COLUMN VIII

... that it (sc. that discipline) is different from [politics], even if it is false that the government of the polis is invariably *not* the rule of one person whereas the government of the property *is* without exception the rule of one person, and (sc. it is false) that there is never an analogy between the two of them. Nor (is it relevant to the discipline of household management) that some of the arts make the products that they use, whereas others do not. At any rate, it is obvious to everybody that it is in the nature of the arts mentioned above both to assemble and then to use (their products). Further, the definition of what the polis is, that too is most evident, as is the claim that the household is constituted before the polis and that, therefore, the discipline of household management is established before the discipline of politics.[29] By contrast, it is a distinctive task of the discipline of household management to count as parts of the household the men and the possessions, and also it is its peculiar

στου φύσιν ἐν τοῖς ἐλαχ[ί]σ[τ]οις
θεωρεῖσθαι, διὸ καὶ τῆς οἰ[κί-
ας]. Καὶ ἄξιον ἐπιζητεῖν πῶς
ἐ[πέ]ζευκται τούτο[ις]· "ὥστε   25
καθ' Ἡσίοδον δέοι ἂν ὑπάρ-
χει]ν 'οἶκον μὲν πρώτιστα
γυν]αῖκά τε·' τὸ μὲν γὰ[ρ] τῆς
τρο]φῆς πρῶτον, τὸ δὲ τῶν
ἐ[λευ]θέρων", εἰ μὴ κτῆσις, ὥσ-   30
περ ἡ] τροφή, γαμετὴ καὶ ταῦ-
τα συ]νοικονομοῦσα· καὶ πῶς
οἶκος τῆ]ς τροφῆς πρῶτο[ν,
κα[ὶ διὰ τί] γυνὴ τῶν ἐλευθέ-
ρω[ν πρῶ]τον, καὶ π[ῶς] δέχε-   35
τα[ι γ]αμετὴν ὑφ' Ἡσιόδου λέ-
γε[σ]θαι τὴν γυναῖκα, πολλῶν
καὶ φασ[κ]όντων αὐτὸν γε-
γραφένα[ι] "κτητήν, οὐ γαμε-
τήν", καὶ τ[ί] τὸ κατὰ φύσιν ε[ἶν]α[ι   40
τὴν γεωργικήν, διὸ πρώτην
ἐπ[ι]μέλειαν αὐτῆς, καὶ πῶς
τὴν μεταλλευτικὴν καὶ πᾶ-
σα[ν τ]ὴν ὁμοίαν σπουδαί-
ων [οἰ]κείαν ὑπολαμβ[άν]ε[ι, κ]αὶ   45
δ]ιὰ [τί] τῶν περὶ ἀνθρ[ωπο]υς

COLUMN IX

τ]ὴν περὶ γαμετὴν πρώτ[ην, γίνεσθαι δυναμένης εὐδαίμο-
νος ζωῆς καὶ χωρὶς αὐτῆς, κα[ὶ
πῶς τὸ τίνα τρόπον γαμετῆ[ι
δεῖ προσφέρεσθαι τ[ῶι] περὶ τῆς   5
σ[υν]ήθως νοουμένης οἰκο-
ν[ο]μίας λόγωι προσήκειν, ὥστε καὶ διὰ τί πάντως δεῖν παρ-
θένον γαμεῖν, καὶ πῶς τῶν
κτημάτων πρῶτον καὶ ἀναγ-   10
καιότατον πρὸς οἰκονομίαν

task that the nature of each of them, and therefore of [the household] as well, should be examined in its smallest details. Moreover, it is worthwhile to inquire further how (Theophrastus) adds to these remarks that "consequently, according to Hesiod, it would be necessary that 'first and foremost there is a house and a woman,' because the one is the principal element of [nourishment] while the other of [free men]," unless the wife is a possession [just like] food, despite being a partner in the management of the household. Also, (it is worthwhile to examine) in what sense [the house] is the principal element of nourishment; [and why] the woman is [the principal element] of free men; and [how] he understands Hesiod's calling the woman "wife," although many people also say that he wrote "acquired, not married";[30] and [what] farming being in accordance with nature, and hence its pursuit being foremost,[31] [consists in]; and in what way he assumes that working in mines and all other similar activity are suitable to good men; and [why], of the preoccupations of the household that deal with people,

COLUMN IX

he assumes the one concerning the wife to be first and foremost, given that there can be a happy life even without her;[32] and how it befits a discourse on property management, if this is understood [in the familiar sense], to study in what way one should approach one's wife, and consequently why one should at all costs marry a virgin; and how of possessions the first and most necessary to the management of the household is the best and the

τὸ βέλτιστον καὶ οἰκονομι-
κώτατον, ὥστ᾽ ἄνθρωπος, καὶ
π[ῶ]ς δούλους πρότερον πα-
ρα[σ]κευαστέον ὧν Ἡσίοδος   15
παραγγέλλει πρώτων, καὶ
π[ῶ]ς δού[λο]υ δύ᾽ εἴδη φησίν,
τ[ὸν] ἐπίτροπον καὶ τὸν ἐργά-
τ[ην], ἀμφοτέρων καὶ ἐλευθέ-
ρων εἶναι δυναμένων, καὶ   20
διὰ [τί] παῖδας κελεύει [π]αρα-
σκε[υα]σάμενον τρέφειν καὶ
παιδεύειν, οἷς τὰ ἐλευθ[έ]ρ[ι]α
τῶν ἔργων προστακτέον,
μᾶ[λλο]ν ἢ πεπαιδευμένους ἤ[13]   25
ὑπ᾽ [ἄλ]λων ἠγμένους*· τ[ὸ] δὲ
[μήθ᾽] ὑβρίζειν ἐᾶν τοὺς δ[ο]ύ-
λ[ους μή]τε π[ι]έζειν καὶ τοῖ[ς
μὲ[ν ἀ]ληθιν[ω]τέροις τιμῆ[ς
με[τα]διδόναι, τοῖς δ᾽ ἐργά-   30
ται[ς τ]ροφῆς πλε[ίο]νος, ἀνε-
κτῶ[ς] εἴρηται· σκληρῶς μέν-
τ[οι] τ[ὴ]ν τοῦ ο[ἴ]νου πόσιν κοιν[ῶς
ἀλλ᾽ [οὐ τὴν] τοῦ πλείονος καὶ
τοὺ[ς] ἐλευθέρους [ὑβ]ριστὰ[ς   35
ποιε[ῖ]ν, διὸ παρὰ πο[λλο]ῖς ἔ-
θνεσ[ι]ν ἀπέχεσθαι, καὶ τούτοις
φανε[ρ]ὸν λέγειν, ὅτι δεῖ δού-
λοις ἢ μηδὲν ἢ ὀλιγάκις με-
ταδιδόναι, φανεροῦ μᾶλλο[ν   40
ὄντος, ὡς ἡ ποσὴ δύναμί[ν
τ᾽ ἐμποεῖ τῆι εὐθυμίαι καὶ χο-
ρηγεῖται παρὰ τοῖς ἐργαστι-
κωτ[έ]ροις. Κοινὰ δὲ κ[αὶ οὐκ ἴ-
δια φ[ιλ]οσόφου τὰ περ[ὶ ἔργου   45
καὶ τ[ρ]οφῆς καὶ κολάσ[εως

---

13. Sedley; <ἤδη καί> Jensen.

most managerial,[33] and hence man; and why one should get slaves before those things that Hesiod recommends providing first; and why he says that there are two kinds of slaves, the bailiff and the workman, who can also both be freemen; and [why] he urges that, having procured them, one bring up and educate slaves to whom one must assign those of the tasks that are fit for freemen, rather than (getting slaves) who have been educated [or] trained by other (slaves). His claims that one should not allow the slaves to run riot and one should not press them and should give responsibility to the more trustworthy among them, but more food to the industrious, are acceptable. However, it is a harsh claim of his that a drink of wine in general, and not just of too much wine, makes even free men insolent (and that this is why many nations abstain from it), and to say that for these reasons it is obvious that one should distribute wine to the slaves either not at all or very seldom, whereas the obvious thing is rather that a certain quantity of wine strengthens the spirit and is in ready supply among those who work most. The instructions concerning their [tasks], nourishment, and punishment are commonplace and

Column X

καὶ] ὑπὸ τῶν μετριωτέρων [φυ-
λαττόμενα· τὸ δ' ἀλόγωι κο-
λάσει μὴ χρῆσθαι καὶ ὁμοίως
λόγωι καὶ ἔργωι προσῆκον μέν,
ἀλλ' οὐ παραληπτέον ἦν ἐν-   5
τα[ῦ]θα περὶ οἰκετῶν χρήσε-
ως· ἢ διὰ τί τοῦτο μόνον; μᾶλλον δὲ καὶ τὰ συναφῆ, διότι
γένη δεῖ πρὸς τὰ ἔργα μήτ' ἄ-
γαν <αἱρεῖσθαι> δειλὰ μήτε θυμικά, καὶ   10
τῶν πόνων ἆθλον προκεῖ-
σθαι, εἰ καὶ τὸ "πᾶσιν" καὶ τὸ
"χρόνον ὁρίζειν" πάντως
οὐ[κ] ἀναγκαῖον, καὶ τὸ "μὴ πολλοὺς ὁμοεθνεῖς". Τὸ δ' ἐξο-   15
μηρεύειν ταῖς τεκνοποι[ί-
α[ις ε]ἰρηκέναι κοινῶς χεῖ-
ρο[ν ε]ἶναι δοκεῖ τοῦ παρὰ Ξε-
νοφῶντι {κελεύειν} τρέφειν
ἐ]κ τῶν ἀγαθῶ[ν], οὐκ ἐκ τῶν   20
πονηρῶν κελεύοντι·* καὶ
τὸ "τὰς εὐθυσίας δὲ καὶ τὰς
ἀπολαύσεις ποιεῖσθαι τῶν
δο[ύ]λων ἕνεκα μᾶλλον ἢ
τῶ[ν] ἐλευθέρων" βιαιότε-   25
ρον ἅμα τῆι πίστει, διότι πλέον [ἔχ]ουσιν, οὗ χάριν τὰ το[ι-
α[ῦτ' ἐ]νομίσθη. Καὶ [ἐ]ν τ[ῶι
τέτ[ταρ]α δ[εῖν] εἶναι τ[ο]ῦ συ[ν-
ήθω[ς ο]ἰκον[όμου προσ]αγο-   30
ρευομένου π[ερὶ τὰ] χρήμ[ατ' εἴδη, τό τ]ε κ[τ]ητι[κὸν κ]αὶ τὸ φ[υ-
λ[ακτικὸν κ]αὶ [τὸ κοσ]μητικ[ὸν
καὶ [τὸ χρηστικὸν ···]ι παρ' ἐ ··
πολλ ·· νοου ···· καταδ ···   35
οταπ ··· τατε ···· ολα[ζ]ειν
αυτον ··· θωσ ··· εχοντος

Column X

observed by the more decent type of person, and they are not the special province of the philosopher. As to the precept that one should not use unreasonable methods of punishment, this does equally concern both theory and practice, but it should not have been taken up here in connection with the treatment of slaves. Otherwise, why should only this point be raised? More in place are the connected matters, namely, that one should not [select] for the tasks (of the estate) races that are either too cowardly or too high-spirited and that a prize should be set as a reward for labors,[34] although the qualifications "to everybody" and "to set a time limit" are certainly not necessary, nor is the saying "not many people of the same race." To affirm, indiscriminately, that one should bind slaves to one's service by letting them have children seems worse than what is found in Xenophon, who recommends breeding children from the good slaves, not from the bad ones. At the same time, too, "to make auspicious sacrifices and to provide enjoyments for the sake of servants rather than for the sake of free men" does more violence to our convictions, "for they (sc. the free) have more possibilities of enjoyment, for the sake of which such things have been instituted." Further, [in the claim that the skills of the man called a property manager according to ordinary usage, which are related to possessions, must be of four kinds, namely, the ability to acquire and to preserve and to arrange and to use] ... nor (is it) the result of prac-

···· σ · μεν οὐδὲ κατὰ τὴν
τέχ[ν]ην, το[ῦ γε] κοσμητικοῦ παρὰ τὸ [κ]τητικὸν καὶ τὸ φυλακτ[ι-   40
κὸν ο[ὐ]κ ὄντος, εἴ γε τὸ τάττειν ὡς δεῖ καὶ ἔνθα δεῖ τοῦτο λα[μ]βάνεται, καθάπερ ἔ-
οικεν· [ἔ]στω δ', εἰ θέλει, κ[αὶ ἡ τέρ-
ψιν ἐ[πι]φέρουσα [τῆι ὠφελίαι   45

COLUMN XI

δ]ιακόσμησις ὑπὸ τὸν οἰκο[νο-
μικόν, ἣν ἀντιδιαιρεῖν ἠξίου
τοῖς ἀναγκαιοτάτοις. Φιλοχρημάτου δὲ τὸ παραινεῖν τῶν
ὑπαρχόντων πλείω τὰ κάρ-   5
πιμ[α] τῶν ἀκάρπων, εἴ γε τὰ
προσοδικὰ καὶ ἀπρόσοδα ταῦ-
τ' ἔλεγεν· εἰ γὰρ τὰ χρήσιμα
καὶ] ἄχρηστα, κοινῶς πάντ' ἔ-
δει χρήσιμα κελεύειν καὶ μη-   10
δὲν ἄχρηστον. Τὸ μέντοι
τὰς ἐργασίας οὕτω νενεμῆ-
σθαι προσήκειν, ὅπως μὴ ἅ-
μα [κ]ινδυνεύῃ πᾶσιν, ἰδιώ-
τηι [μ]ὲν παραινούμενον λό-   15
γον ἔχει, φιλόσοφος δ' οὔτ' ἐρ-
γάζεται, κυρίως εἰπεῖν, οὔτ', ἂν
ἐρ[γά]σηταί ποτε, πᾶσι [φ]αίνε-
τα[ι κιν]δυνεύειν, ὥστε πα-
ρα[κελε]ύσεως τοῦ μὴ ποεῖν   20
δ]εῖσθ[α]ι· τῆ[ς] δὲ φυλακῆς, ἥν
γ]ε Ἀτ[τι]κή[ν] φησιν εἶναι, "πω-
λοῦντας ὠνεῖσθαι", δυσχε-
ρ[ής, τ]άχα δὲ καὶ ἀλυσιτελής·
καὶ [τ]ῆς Περσικῆς τὸ πάντ' αὐ-   25
τὸν] ἐφορᾶν· γνωστὸν δὲ
πᾶ]σιν τὸ δεῖν ἐπιβλέπειν ἀεὶ
μὲν ἐ]ν οἰκονομίαι μικρᾶι,

ticing an art, since the capacity of arranging does not exist over and above the capacities of acquiring and of preserving, if at any rate arrangement is taken to mean, as it does seem to mean, arranging the possessions as one should and where one should. But let us grant, if he (sc. Theophrastus) wishes, that the process of arranging that adds enjoyment to the utility,

COLUMN XI

which he saw fit to contradistinguish from the bare essentials (sc. the acquisition, preservation, and use), falls under the property manager.[35] Nonetheless, it is the mark of a mercenary person to advise having a greater quantity of "fruitful" than of "unfruitful" possessions—if, at any rate, by these he meant lucrative and unlucrative. For if instead he meant useful and useless in general, he should have recommended that everything be useful and nothing useless. That it is appropriate to have distributed the tasks so as not to endanger all the possessions at once is, of course, good advice for an ordinary person. But the philosopher, properly speaking, does not work, nor, if he ever works, does he seem to put everything at risk so as [to need exhortation] not to do it. Regarding the manner of preserving the property that he claims to be Attic, namely, "to purchase at the same time as one sells," it is troublesome and perhaps also unprofitable, and the same holds for the precept of watching over everything oneself that is a characteristic of the Persian method.[36] Besides, everybody knows that one must always inspect things in a small property

πολλά]κις δ' ἐν ἐπιτροπευ-
ομένηι·] ταλαίπωρον δὲ καὶ   30
ἀνοί[κε]ιον φιλοσόφου τὸ
πρότ[ερ]ον τῶν οἰκετῶν ἐ-
γε[ίρεσθ]αι καὶ καθεύδειν ὕστε-
ρο[ν· φα]νερὸν δὲ καὶ το[ῖ]ς τυ-
χοῦσ[ιν τὸ μ]ηδέποθ' ὅλην   35
οἰκία[ν] ἀφ[ύλα]κτον εἶναι, πά-
νυ δ' ἐ[πί]πονον τὸ δ[ιαν]ίστα-
σθαι νύκτωρ εἰωθέναι· ζ[η-
τῶ δ' ε[ἰ] καὶ πρὸς ὑγίειαν καὶ
φιλοσοφ[ί]α[ν] ἐν ταῖς μικραῖς   40
συμφέρει νυξίν. Εἰ δὲ καὶ π[ερὶ
τοῦ] φρουροῦ τὸν φιλόσοφον
δ]εῖ παραγγέλλειν προστι-
θ]έντ[α τ]ὸ "σωτηρίας ἕνεκα
τῶ]ν [εἰσ]φερομένων καὶ ἐκ-   45
φερομέ]νων" καὶ τὸ "τοῦτον
ἄχρηστ]ον εἶναι τῶν ἄλλω[ν

Column XII

ἔρ]γων", καὶ τοῦτο θεματ[ίζω-
με[ν]. Τὰ μὲν οὖν πρὸς τούτους
ἱκανῶς ἐπισεσήμανται, τὰ δ' ἡ-
μῖν ἀρέσκοντα συντόμως
ὑπο[γρα]πτέον. Διαλεξόμε-   5
θα τ[ο]ίνυν οὐχ ὡς ἐν οἴκωι κα-
λῶ[ς] ἔστιν βιοῦν, ἀλλ' ὡς ἵστα-
σθαι δεῖ περὶ χρημάτων κτή-
σεώς τε καὶ φυλακῆς, περὶ [ἃ
τὴν οἰκονομίαν καὶ τὸν   10
οἰκονομικὸν ἰδίως νοεῖσθαι
συμβέβηκεν, οὐδὲν διαφε-
ρόμενοι πρὸς τοὺς ἕτερα τοῖς
ὀν[ό]μασιν ὑποτάττειν προ-
αιρ[ο]υμένους, καὶ περὶ τῆς   15
φιλοσόφωι δεούσης κτήσε-
ως, [οὐ] τῆς ὁτωι[δή]ποτε. Φι-

and must do so [very often in a property run by a bailiff]. However, [to wake up] before the servants and to go to sleep after them is wretched and unfitting for the philosopher. Besides, it is clear even to ordinary people that the house is never completely [unguarded], and it is very bothersome to acquire the habit of [getting up] in the course of the night. In fact, I am wondering if this activity, (when practiced) in the short nights of the year, is good for health and for the study of philosophy. And if the philosopher has also to give advice about the custodian, adding the qualifications "for the safekeeping of all possessions carried into the household and [out of it]" and "he (sc. the custodian) [is not to be used] for other

Column XII

works," let us recognize this too as a topic.

Thus, the answers to these authors have been indicated well enough, but we ought to outline briefly our own views.[37] We shall discuss, then, not how one can live well at home but what attitude one must take up both with regard to the acquisition and the preservation of wealth, concerning which property management and the property-management expert are in fact conceived specifically, (and we shall do so) without contending at all with those who prefer to make other meanings underlie the terms and, moreover, discussing the acquisition (of property) that is appropriate for the philosopher, [not] for just anyone. Well, there is for

λοσό]φωι δ' ἐστὶ πλούτου
μέ[τρ]ον, ὃ παρεδώκαμεν
ἀκολ]ο[ύ]θως τοῖς καθηγε-　　　　　20
μόσιν] ἐν τοῖς Περὶ π[λού]του
λόγο]ις, ὥστε τὴν οἰκον[ομι-
κὴ]ν τῆς τε τούτου κ[τή]σε-
ως κ]αὶ τῆς τούτου φυλ[ακ]ῆς
ἀποδ]ίδοσθαι. Κεῖται τοί-　　　　　25
ν[υν ἐ]ν τῶι Περὶ πλού[το]υ
Μ[ητρ]οδώρου τοιαῦτα πρὸς
τ[ὸν τό]πον ἐν τῶι λόγωι τῶι
π[ρὸς τ]οὺς ἐροῦντας ἴσως
ὅ[τι πολ]ὺ κουφοτάτην καὶ　　　　　30
ῥά[ι]σ[τη]ν οἱ Κυνικοὶ διαγωγὴν [ᾕρην]ται πᾶν αὑτῶν πε-
ριε[ιρηκό]τες εἰς τὸ δυνατόν,
ὃ μ[ή γ' εὐ]τελῆ παρέχει βίον
εἰρη[ναίως τ]ε καὶ μάλιστ' ἀ-　　　　　35
θορύβ[ω]ς [καὶ μετὰ τῆ]ς ἐλα-
χίστη[ς] φρο[ντίδος κ]αὶ πρα-
γματε[ί]ας [δια]νυ[ό]μενον· ὅ-
πε[ρ] ἔχ[ει]ν τὸν α[ὑ]τὸ μόνον
τὸ κ]αθ' ἡ[μέραν π]οριζόμε-　　　　　40
νον·] τοῦτο γὰρ [εἶ]ναι καὶ πρὸς
φιλό]σοφον, τὸ δὲ πλέον τούτου π]ᾶν ἤδη κενόν· [γ]έγρα-
φεν οὖν,] ὡς τοῦτο μ[ὲ]ν ἀρέ-
σκει λέγ]ειν, ὅτι βίος οὗτος　　　　　45
ἄρισ]το[ς], ὧι ἡ πλε[ίστ]η συν[παρέ-

Column XIII

πεθ' ἡσυχί]α καὶ εἰρήνη καὶ [ἐλα-
χίστη παρενοχλοῦσα φρον-
τίς· οὐ μὴν οὕτω γε φαίνεται
τοῦτο γίνεσθαι τὸ τέλος, ἂν
πάντα φύγωμεν, ὧν ὑπαρ-　　　　　5
χ[όν]των κἂν πράγματά πο-
τε σχῶμεν κἂν ἀγωνιάσαι-

the philosopher a measure of wealth[38] that, [following] the founders of the school, we have passed down in [the treatise] *On Wealth*, so as to render an account of the art of managing the acquisition of this and the preservation of this. Now, such pertinent views are found in Metrodorus's treatise *On Wealth*, in argument [against those] who might claim that the Cynics [have chosen] a way of life that is [by far] the lightest and [easiest], since they [have stripped off] from themselves, to the extent that this is possible, everything that does [not] yield a frugal life [led peacefully] and without any disturbance at all, [as well as with the least possible care and labor].[39] [And (he says) that this is the very thing obtained by the man who provides for himself only what he needs day by day]; for this in fact is sufficient also for the philosopher, whereas anything more than this is completely useless. He (sc. Metrodorus) [writes] that, although he likes the idea that the [best] life is the one that is [accompanied]

Column XIII

[by tranquillity], peace, and cares that cause minimal trouble, it does not seem that this goal is achieved at least in this way, namely, if we avoid all those things over which, if they were present, we would sometimes experience difficulties and distress. For in truth many things do cause

μεν. Πολλὰ γὰρ τῶν πραγμάτων ἐνποεῖ μέν τινας λύπας
ὑπάρχοντα, πλείω δ᾽ ὀχλεῖ   10
μὴ παρόντα. Τὸ δ᾽ οὖν ὑγιαί-
νειν τῶι σώματι φροντίδα
μὲν ἔχει τινὰ καὶ πόνον, ἀ-
πλάτωι μέντοι μᾶλλον, ὅταν
ἀ[πῆι], χειμάζει{ν}.¹⁴ Πα[ρα]πλησί-   15
ως δὲ κα[ὶ] ὁ βέβαιος φίλο[ς] ἐν-
ποιῶν [τ]ινας ὑπ[άρχων π]ου λ[ύ-
π[ας] πλείω μὴ ὑπάρχων ἐνο-
χλ[ε]ῖ. Τοιοῦτος [γ]ὰ[ρ] δῆλ[ο]ν
ὡς [ὁ σ]που[δ]αῖος, οἷο[ς π]ολλὰ   20
τῶι συμφ[έ]ροντι κα[ὶ ἀ]συμ-
φόρωι δ[ιορ]ίζων [ἑλέσθαι] μᾶλλο[ν] ἑτέρ[ω]ν ἔτε[ρα, καὶ μ]ὴ
τοῦτο ποιῶν οὐ δε[ξι]ῶ[ς], οὐ-
χ ὅτ[ι] καλῶς ζῆν δύνασθαι,   25
καὶ [π]ροσδεῖσθαί τε πολλῶν,
ἃ μ[ὴ κ]εκτημένος [βι]ώσεται
ἐμπα]θεστέρως, [κα]ὶ στ[ερό-
μ[ενο]ς ἐνίων ὀχλεῖ[σ]θ[αι. Π]άν-
τα [μὲ]ν οὖν οὐ φευ[κ]τέον, ὧν   30
ὑπα[ρχό]ντων καὶ πρ[άγ]ματα
ἔχει[ν] ἔστιν καὶ φροντίδ[α]ς
καὶ [ἀγ]ωνίας οἱασδήποτε, ὡς
προείπαμεν· τινὰ δὲ
δεχ[τέον], ὧν καὶ τὸν πλοῦ-   35
τον, τ[ὸ] βάρος ἔχοντα με[ῖ-
ον ὅταν παρῆι, μᾶλλον π[ρ]ὸς
ὅλον [βί]ον ἀλλὰ μὴ πρός τ[ι]να
καιρό[ν]· τὸ δ᾽ αὐτῶ[ι χρ]ῆσθα[ι] κα-
νόνι τῶι [π]όνους [ἔχειν] οὐκ ἀ-   40
σφαλές· κα[ὶ] γὰρ τῷ [ποριζομέ-
νῳ τὸ καθ᾽ ἡμέραν [εἰσὶ πόνοι,
καί ποτε [ὀ]χλήσει[ς τι]νὰς

---

14. Sedley; χειμάζειν Jensen.

some pain if they are present but disturb us more if they are absent. Thus, health does involve some care and effort for the body but causes unspeakably more distress when it is absent. And in a similar way the faithful friend also, who perhaps causes some [pains when he exists], distresses us more when he does not exist. In fact, it is clear that the good person is the kind of person who, [differentiating] many things by reference to what is profitable and what is not profitable, [chooses some things rather than others] and who, if he does not do this, cannot live [competently], let alone decorously and, moreover, who both needs many things without the possession of which he will lead a more [perturbed] life and is distressed [when he is deprived] of certain things. So, as we have said above,[40] one must not avoid all things that, if they are present, may cause all kinds of troubles, concerns, and worries. On the contrary, [one must accept] some things, among which is in fact wealth, that are less of a burden when they are present, much more so for one's entire life and not only for some specific occasion. Furthermore, the presence of toils as one's actual criterion is not an unfailing guide. For in fact the person who [provides for himself] day by day [is subject to toils], and also the big spender is sometimes

ὁ δαψι[λε]ύων ἔχει· [παραπλη-
σίως [δὲ] καὶ τῶι τὰ β[ρ]αχέα¹⁵   45
κ]εκτημένωι δίκα[ιον μηδὲ

COLUMN XIV

ταῦτ' ἀποδοκιμάσαι δι[ὰ τὴν
τοιαύτην συντυ[χί]αν, τὸ δ' ὡς
ἐπὶ τὸ πολὺ συνεργοῦν πρὸς
τὴν ἀκροτάτην δι[α]γωγὴν
τοῦτο σκεπτέον. Οὐ φαίνε-   5
ται δ' ὁ πλοῦτος ἐπιφέρειν ἀ-
λυσιτελεῖς δυσχερείας παρ' αὐτὸν ἀλλὰ παρὰ τὴ[ν] τῶν χρω-
μένων κακίαν. Ἡ γὰρ ἐπιμέ-
λεια καὶ τήρησις, ὅση πρέπει   10
τῶι κατὰ τρόπον αὐτοῦ προ-
εστῶτι, παρέχει μέν τιν' ἐνί-
οτ' ὄχλησιν, οὐ μὴν πλείω
γε τοῦ κατὰ τὸν ἐφήμερον
πο]ρισμόν, ἂν δὲ καὶ πλείω,   15
τῶν ἄλ[λ]ων ὧν ἀπαλλάτ-
τει δυσχερῶν [ο]ὐ πλείον', ἂν
μ[ὴ] δείξῃ τις ὡς οὐκ ἀποδί-
δω]σιν ὁ φυσικὸς πλοῦτος
πο]λλῶ[ι] μείζους τὰς ἐπικαρ-   20
πίας ἢ τοὺς πόνους τῆς ἀπ' [ὀ-
λίγων ζωῆς, ὃ πολλοῦ δεή-
σε[ι παρ]ιστάνε[ιν. Τ]ῶι γὰρ μὴ
λυ[πε]ῖσθαι τ[ῶι] παραπολλυμέ-
ν[ωι] μηδὲ διὰ τὴν ἄκρατον   25
σ[που]δὴν περὶ τὸ πλέον καὶ
το[ὔλαττ]ον ὑφ' αὑ[τ]οῦ ζητρί-
οις τισὶ]ν ἐ[γκ]εῖσθαι, τούτω[ι
γ'] ὀ[ρ]θῶς οἰκο[νο]μεῖσθαι νο-
μίζω τὸν πλοῦ[τ]ον· ὁ [γ]ὰρ κατὰ   30

_____

15. Delattre, Tsouna; [μέτρια] Jensen.

subject to certain troubles. And similarly, it is also not right for the person who has acquired a [small] amount of possessions

Column XIV

to reject even them on account of a change of fortune of this kind, but instead one should consider the thing that contributes for the most part to the most perfect way of life. Wealth does not seem to bring profitless difficulties through itself but rather through the wickedness of those who use it. For the degree of diligence and vigilance that are fitting for the person who manages it in the proper manner sometimes do give some trouble, but certainly not greater than that involved in providing what is necessary day by day. But even if it is greater than that, it is not greater than the [other] difficulties that it removes, unless one can demonstrate that natural wealth does *not* secure profits much greater than the toils of the frugal life—something that [it would take a lot to prove]. Indeed, I think[41] that the right management of wealth lies in this: in not feeling distressed about what one loses and in not [trapping oneself on treadmills] because of an obsessive [zeal] concerning the more and the less. For the pain involved in the [acquisition] of wealth consists both in eking out [a

τὴ[ν κτῆ]σ[ι]ν π[όν]ος [κἂν] τῶι
προ[σφορ]ὰν ἕλκειν ἑαυ[τῷ]¹⁶ γί-
νετ[αι] κἂν τῶι περὶ τῶν ἐλατ-
τ[ὶωμάτ]ων ἀγωνιᾶν ὡς εὐ-
θέ[ως εἰ]ς ἀλγηδόν[α κ]α[τ]α-   35
στησόντων ἢ παροῦσαν ἢ
προσδοκωμένην. Ἂν δέ τις
περι[έ]λη[ι] ἑαυτοῦ τὰς τοι[α]ύ-
τας [δ]υσχερείας καὶ μὴ [σ]ω-
ρεύειν ἐπιβάλ[η]ται καὶ πο-   40
εῖν τὴν οὐσίαν ὅτι μεγίστην,
μηδ᾽ ἢν ὁ πλο[ῦ]τος ἐξουσί-
αν παρέχει τα[ύ]την παρασκευ-
άζη[τ]αι τῶι δ[υ]σχερῶς αὐ-
τὸς [τ]ὰ χρήματα φυλάτ[τειν ἢ συν-   45
άγε[ιν] λιπαρῶς, ἀπαρά[λλα-

COLUMN XV

κτος γίνοιτ᾽ ἂν διὰ [ταῦτα]¹⁷
ἑτοιμότης τῆς κτήσεως τῆι
καὶ δι᾽ αὐτοῦ κοινωνούσηι· διοικεῖν γὰρ οὕτω ταῦτα τῶι κε-
κτῆσθαι καὶ κτᾶσθαι τὸν σο-   5
φὸν φίλους ἀκόλουθον· προσ-
έτι δὲ μὴ διακέηται τὸν τρόπον τοῦτον, ὡς ἐὰν ἀναλω-
θῇ ταῦτ᾽, ἄλλων οὐχ εὑρεθη-
σομένων, πολλή τις γίνε-   10
ται ῥαιστώνη περὶ τὴν οἰκο-
νομίαν, ἄλλως τε καὶ τοῖς †
<δεδιόσι>¹⁸ κοινώνημα λόγων δεόμε-

---

16. Delattre; πρὸ[ς βί]αν ἕλκειν ἑαυ[τὸν] Jensen.
17. Sedley; δία[ιτα καὶ Jensen. On Jensen's construction the text has an
entirely different meaning: "one's [life] would acquire stability as would the
ready availability of one's property for the life that shares through him as
well" (XV.1–3).
18. <δεδιόσι> Sedley; Jensen om.

profit for oneself][42] and in agonizing over one's losses on the grounds that they will bring one directly into pain, whether present or expected. But if one has removed from oneself such difficulties and does not eagerly desire to amass and make one's property as great as possible and, moreover, does not procure for oneself those resources that wealth offers by oneself watching painfully over one's possessions or [by collecting] them in rich abundance,

Column XV

[as a result of this] a readiness for acquisition would become indistinguishable from one's readiness to share things very much on one's own initiative.[43] In truth, that the wise man administers these goods in such a manner is a consequence of the fact that he has acquired and continues to acquire friends. Moreover, one should not be disposed in such a manner that, if these goods are consumed and if no other resources are destined to be found, there will be a lot of indolence regarding financial matters, [especially for those who fear[44] an exchange of arguments that

[νο]ν[19] πολλῶν ἀγώνων· ἂν δέ
που καὶ περιπέσωσι τοι-   15
ούτωι δυνάμενοι μηδὲ
ἕν]α φιλονεικεῖν πλὴν θορύ-
β]ου κερδαίνοντας, ἐλαττοῦ-
ται τὰ[20] λυσιτελῆ[21] πρὸς τὸ τέλος, οὗ χάριν καὶ πλ[ε]ονε[κ]τεῖν   20
βουλόμενοι· λέγειν γὰρ [ἔξ-
εστι]ν ὡς ὁ τοιοῦτος ἔχ[ει
ῥᾶιον κτ]ῆσιν ἐφήμερον οὕτως
ἀνειμένος ὢν περὶ τὰ ῥηθέν-
τα] τοῦ μηδὲν ἐφόδιον ἔχον-   25
τ[ο]ς· οὐ γὰρ ἧτ[τ]ον ὁρῶμεν τὰς
τῶ]ν τοιούτων οὐσ[ί]ας σῳζο-
μέ]νας ἢ τὰς τῶν [ἐν]τό[νων,
ε[ἰ] δὲ μή γ', οὐχ οὕτ[ω τα]χέως
φ[θειρο]μένας οὐδ' [ἴσ]ως ἀκρο-   30
σφ[αλ]εῖς οὔσας. Ἐνδεθήσε-
τ[αι μ]ὲν οὖν οὐδέποθ' οὕτως
ὑπὸ π]λούτου σοφὸς ἀνήρ, ὥσ-
θ' ἕνεκ]α τοῦ δι[α]σῴζειν αὐτὸν μεγάλους ὑπομένειν   35
πό[ν]ους καὶ πρὸς οὐδὲν πλῆ-
θος ἀλλακτούς· τοῦτο γὰρ
δε[ῖ] καὶ ποεῖν τὴν χρείαν ἄ-
λυπον καὶ τὸ διὰ ταύτης τέρ-
πον ἀκέραιον τὸ μὴ προσεῖ-   40
ναι τῆι πλούτου κτήσει τοῖς
σοφοῖς φροντίδα βαρεῖαν,
πῶς δυνήσεται σῴζεσθαι,
μη[δ'] ὅταν οἱ σφαλερώ[τ]ατοι
κ[αιρ]οὶ καθεστήκωσι[ν· οὔ-   45
τε [γ]ὰρ ἀσχαλᾶι σώφρων ἀ-

---

19. Sedley; δεομέ-|νω]ν Jensen.
20. Sedley; ἐλαττοῦ-|σθ]αί τε Jensen.
21. Göttling; τε λυσιτελῆ Jensen.

requires a lot of disputes].[45] And, no doubt, if they encounter something of this kind, and are not able to engage in dispute with anyone other than people who make their gains at the cost of noise, there is a diminution in the things that are conducive to the end for whose sake they actually want to profiteer. Now, [it is possible] to maintain that this kind of man (sc. the sage), relieved in that manner (of his worries) about the matters mentioned above, [has an easier time in acquiring] what is necessary day by day than the one who does not have any resource whatsoever. In the event, we observe that the estates of such people are not preserved any less than those [of assiduous property managers,] or in any case that they are at least not [ruined] so fast and that, [perhaps], they are not so precarious either. The wise man will never be bound by wealth in such a way as to endure, [in order to] preserve it, toils that are great and are not such as to be exchanged for any quantity of wealth. For what makes its use painless and the enjoyment deriving from it pure must be this, the fact that for sages no heavy care about how it will be possible to preserve it is attached to the possession of wealth, not even when [circumstances] become most critical. So neither does a moderate person,

Column XVI

νὴρ καὶ πρὸς τὸ μέλλ[ον εὐ]θ[α]ρ-
ρὴς τῆι ταπεινῆι καὶ πενιχρᾶι
διαίτηι, τὸ φυσικὸν εἰδὼς καὶ ὑ-
πὸ ταύτης διοικούμενον, ῥέπει
δὲ τῆι βουλήσει μᾶλλον ἐπὶ   5
τὴν ἀφθονωτέραν, οὔτε κ[α-
κὸς εὑρέσθαι τὰ πρὸς αὐτὸν
ἱκανά, ὧι καὶ βίος μέτριός τε
καὶ κοινὸς καὶ λόγος ὑγιὴς καὶ
ἀληθινός, εἰ καὶ μὴ ῥαιδίως   10
τὸν τυχόντα προσαγόμε-
νος. Τίνος ἂν οὖν ἕνεκα τη-
λικαῦτ' ἔχων ἐφόδια πρὸς τὸ
ζῆν καλῶς ἐν πολλῆι ῥαισ[τώ-
νηι, κἂν πλοῦτον ἀποβάληι,   15
πέραι τοῦ μετρίου κακοπα-
θήσει σωτηρίας ἕνεκ[α χ]ρ[η-
μάτων; οὐ μὴν ἀλλ' οὐδ' [ἀ-
κροσφα[λ]ῶς αὑτῶι διακείσ[ε-
ται τὰ ὑπάρχονθ' ο[ἵ]ωι π[ρο]είπα-   20
μεν ὄντι· καὶ γὰρ οὐδὲ [κ]α-
κὸν οἰκονόμον ἐρεῖ τις εἶναι κατὰ τὴν χρείαν αὐτὸν οὐ-
δέ τ[οι τ]ὴν [δι]οίκησίν τε καὶ
φυλακή[ν· ἀβ]έλτερον γάρ ἐ[στι   25
τὸ μὴ [σώζειν], ἐφ' ὅσον μήτε
πόνος παρὰ τὸ προσῆκον
γίνεται μήτε τῶν δεόντ[ων
ἀ]ναλωθῆναί τι παραλεί-
πε]ται, φυσικῶν ἡμῖν ἐνόν-   30
τ]ων πρὸς τὰ πλείον' ἐπιθ[υ]-
μιῶν,²² οὐ[δὲ] ῥαιδίω[ς ο]ἶκον ο[ἰ-
κον]ομῶ[ν] μετ' α[ὐ]τοῦ τοῦ
λόγ]ο[υ κ]αὶ {αὐτοῦ [τ]οῦ λόγου

---

22. Tsouna; ἐπιτ···|·μων Jensen.

Column XVI

[full of good courage] toward the future in virtue of his humble and modest way of living, become distressed, since he knows that what is natural is actually provided by that mode of life, but nonetheless he feels more inclined by his will toward a more affluent way of living,[46] nor is he lazy in getting for himself what is sufficient for him, he whose way of life is moderate and communal and whose reasoning doctrine is healthy and true, even if it does not easily attract just anybody. On account of what, then, would he stress himself beyond measure in order to preserve his possessions, since he has such resources for living well in great ease even if he should lose his wealth?[47] Nevertheless, given that he is the kind of man that we described above, his belongings will not even be in an insecure condition. Nor indeed will anybody call him a *bad* property manager in the use, nor [yet] in the administration and the preservation, of wealth. For it is stupid not [to preserve our wealth] in so far as neither is any unseemly labor involved nor do we omit to spend anything of what must be spent, since there are within us natural desires for more goods.[48] Nor will he fail in his task, [if he administers] his estate with ease by aid of [reason] itself and of the [common] experience that is adequate for the manage-

κ[αὶ] κοι]ν[ῆ]ς ἐμπειρίας τῆς   35
ἱκανῆς π[ρὸς τὴν οἰ]κονομί-
αν τ[ῶ]ν ὑπαρχόν[τ]ων καὶ μὴ
πρὸς ὑπέρμετρο[ν] χρηματι-
σμὸν ὑστερήσει· ῥάιδιον γὰρ
ἰδεῖν παντὶ τὰ κατ[ὰ τ]οῦτο   40
χρήσιμα καὶ ἐν μέσωι κείμε-
να μὴ σωρευταῖς ἀνθρώ[ποις,
ἀ[λ]λ' αὐτὴν τὴν ὑπάρχουσ[αν
κτῆσ]ιν οἰκονομοῦσιν, τὸ [δὲ
π]λεῖον, ἃ[ν ἀ]βλ[α]βῶς καὶ [εὐ-   45
πόρως γίνηται, δεκτέ[ον, τὸ

Column XVII

δὲ κακοπαθ[ε]ῖν [κατ' α]ὐτὸ τοῦτο μή προειρημένοις. Τεχνίτης μὲν οὖν ἅμα καὶ ἐργάτης
κ]τήσεως πολλῆς καὶ ταχέ-
ως συναγομένης οὐκ ἴσως   5
ῥητέος ὁ σοφός· ἔστι γὰρ δή
τις ἐμπειρία καὶ δύναμις καὶ
περὶ χρηματισμόν, ἧς οὐ κοι-
νωνήσει σπουδαῖος ἀ[ν]ήρ,
οὐδὲ τοὺς καιροὺς παρατη-   10
ρήσει, μεθ' ὧν κἂν ἡ τοιαύ-
τη δύναμις χρησίμη γί-
νοιτο· φιλοχρημάτου γὰρ ἅ-
παντα τοιαῦτα. Οὐ μὴν ἀλλὰ
φαίνεταί γε καθάπερ [καὶ] ἐ-   15
π' ἄλλων πλειόνων, ἐν οἷς ἀ-
γαθῶν ὄντων δημιουργῶν
τό γε [πρ]ὸς τὴν χρείαν [ἀρ-
κοῦν ἕκαστος ἡμῶν, [ὡς] εἰ-
πεῖν, οὐ κακῶς <ἂν> ἐπιτελώηι·   20
οἷον ὁρῶμεν καὶ [περ]ὶ τὴν
τοῦ σίτου κατεργασίαν ἢ τὴν
τῶν ὄψων σκε[υ]ασίαν· πᾶς
γάρ τις ἱκανὸς α[ὑ]τῶι τὰ τοι-

ment of one's possessions, though not for excessive moneymaking. For it is easy for everyone to discern the things that, according to this criterion, are useful and lie within reach for people who do not heap up wealth but who manage the actual [property] that they have. As to greater wealth, if it comes [in a harmless and easy manner], then it is to be welcomed;

COLUMN XVII

but to suffer [on account of that very thing] should not be tolerated for the reasons mentioned above.[49] Thus, perhaps the wise man cannot be called in equal measure at one and the same time an expert and a producer of possessions collected in great quantity and in a short time. For in fact there is an empirical practice and ability specially related also to money-making, of which a good man will not have a share, nor will he watch the opportunities in combination with which even this kind of ability could be useful. For all these things characterize the person who loves money.[50] Nevertheless, (what holds in this case) at any rate appears to be exactly like what holds in the case of several other practices in which, although there exist good professional workmen, each one of us could accomplish quite well, as it were, at least what is sufficient for our needs.[51] We observe this, for example, in the production of bread or in the preparation of food. For everybody is able to make such things for himself to the point of meeting

αὖτα ποιεῖν μέχρι τῆς [ἀ]ρ-   25
κούσης χρεία[ς], οὔσης [περ]ὶ
αὐτὰ καὶ ἐνπειρίας ἐν[τέ]χνου.
Καὶ ἐπὶ κτήσεως οὖν [καὶ φυ-
λα[κ]ῆς [τ]ῶν χρημάτ[ων φαί-
νεταί τ[ι τ]οιοῦτον εἶναι. κ[ἂν   30
γὰρ μὴ ὦ[μ]εν τεχνῖται, [κα-
θάπερ τινές, συναγωγῆ[ς κ]αὶ
τηρήσεως καὶ φροντιστα[ὶ σ]ύν-
τονοι καὶ ἐνδελεχεῖς, [ἀλλὰ
μέχρι γε τοῦ τὰ πρὸς τὴν [χρ]εί-   35
αν ἐξευρίσκειν καὶ ταύτ[ηι
μὴ διαπίπτειν εἰκῇ καὶ τ[ελέ-
ως ἐοίκασι πολλοί τινες ο[ὐ-
κ ὄντες κακοί, ὧν καὶ τὸν σ[πο]υ-
δα[ῖ]ον ἄνδρα [ῥητ]έον· τί γάρ²³·   40
κἂν αὐτὸν ἀπ[οφῶ]σι τοιοῦ-
τον ὑπάρχειν, ἀλλ' οὐ κατά
γε τὸ διατ[α]κτικ[ὸ]ν καὶ παρα-
μετρητι[κ]ὸν τῶι φ[υσ]ικῶι
τέλει τοῦ δέον[τ]ος ἥ[ττω] εἶ-   45
ναι· κἂν ὧδ' εἰπῶσ[ι π]ορισθῆ-
ναι²⁴ καὶ μηθὲν ἔξω τοῦ χρη-

Column XVIII

σίμου πεσε[ῖσθαι, τ]ὸ πᾶν διαφέρειν τῶν ἄλλων ῥητέον· ἔτι
δὲ κατὰ τὸ παραστατικὸν
ἀνθρώπων ἀπὸ τοῦ πρὸς τὰ
ὀλία θάρσους διὰ τῶν τοῦ σο-   5
φοῦ λόγων εἰς τὸ παντὸς με-
ταδότας γίνεσθαι. Μὴ δὴ
λέγωμεν ὡς, εἰ περιαιρήσο-
μεν τὸ βάρος αὐτοῦ κατὰ τὴν

---

23. τί γάρ Delattre; Jensen om.
24. Sedley; εἴπωσ[ιν] ὁρισθῆ-|ναι Jensen.

sufficient needs, although there is an empirical practice involving expertise [about] them as well. Now, it seems that something like this holds also
regarding the acquisition and preservation of property. For even if we are
not, like certain people, experts in amassing and preserving wealth nor
earnest and persevering managers of property, [nonetheless] there seem
to be many persons who are not bad at this, at least to the point of finding
what they need and not [totally] failing in this matter by acting randomly.
The good man too must be counted among these people. [Why], even if
they [deny] that he is that kind of person, they certainly cannot (mean)
that he is [worse] than he should be regarding classification and measure-
ment in accordance with the natural end. And even if they say that this is
how things [have been provided] and that none of them [will fall] outside
what is useful,

Column XVIII

we must retort that he is different from the others (sc. the expert managers) in every respect. And, what is more, (he differs from the other
experts) regarding his capacity to exhort men to share all their wealth
(freely), inspired by his confidence in the adequacy of few possessions and
assisted by the discourses of the sage. Let us not say, then, that if we lift off
him the burden related to the acquisition of property, we shall also take

κτῆσιν, ἀφελούμεθα καὶ τὸ   10
πλουτεῖν· ἔστι γὰρ μὴ προσ-
όντος ἐκείνου τοῦτο κατα-
λείπειν· οὐδὲ γὰρ τοῖς συντο-
νωτάτοις παρὰ τὴν περὶ τὸ
πρᾶγμα ταλαιπωρί[α]ν σῴζε-   15
ται μόνως, ἀλλ' αὕτη μὲν τὰ
πολλὰ συνπαρ[έ]πετ' αὐτοῖς,
ἡ δὲ σωτηρία δύν[ατ]αι γίνεσθαι καὶ χωρὶς τῶν [μ]αταίων
πόνων.* Οὔπω γὰρ εἰ περιείρη-   20
κέ τις ἑαυτο[ῦ τό] τε πρὸς μη-
δὲν ἄλογον κακοπαθεῖν
ἐν ταῖς ἐπιμελείαις καὶ τὴν
δυσχερῆ φροντίδα περ[ὶ τ]ῶν
ὑπαρχόντ[ω]ν, ο[ὐ κα]ταλέλοι-   25
πεν τοσοῦ[τ]ον ἑαυτῶι τὸ δι-
αφέρον ἐν τῶι σῴζεσθαι τὴν
κτῆσιν ἢ μὴ σῴζε[σθα]ι, ὃ γε-
νήσεθ' ἱκανὸν πρ[ὸς τ]ὴν σω-
τηρίαν το[ῦ] πλούτου [καὶ φυ]λα-   30
κήν.* Οἷον μὲγ γὰρ τὸ[ν] ἀγα-
θὸν ἐργάτην καὶ φύ[λα]κα κτήσεως οἱ πολλ[οὶ] λέγο[υσ]ιν, οὐ-
δὲ τὸ φιλάνθρωπ[ον <ἀποδέχονται>²⁵ κ]αὶ με-
ταδοτικὸν πρὸς τῶι ταῦτ' ἀ-   35
γνοεῖν ὧν οὔκ εἰσιν ἀρ[ι]θ[μοί
τινες· οὐ γὰρ ῥάιδιον τ[ὸ]ν τοι-
οῦτον ἐξ ὀλίγων πο[λλ]ὰ
ποιεῖν οὐδὲ ποήσαντ[α σῴζ]ειν.
Μετρήσει μὲν οὖν ἴσω[ς τὸ   40
συμφέρον καὶ κτήσει καὶ
φυλακῆι πολὺ βέλτισθ' οὗτος,
ὥστε μὴ πλείω [π]ονεῖν δι-
ὰ τὰ χρήματ' ἤπερ εὐπαθεῖν·
οὔτε γὰρ ὁ πόνος ὁ καθ' ὁποι-   45

---

25. <ἀποδέχονται> Sudhaus, Jensen; Tsouna om.

his wealth away from him. For we can leave him with the latter even if the former is not present. Nor does the most assiduous managers' preservation of their wealth depend solely on struggling over their business: although this accompanies most of their activities, the preservation of wealth can also be obtained without useless labors. In fact, if a person has lifted off himself the suffering involved in his activities concerning worthless things, and also the vexatious care about his belongings, he has not yet failed to leave himself a big enough difference, in the question of his property's being preserved or not preserved, to suffice for the preservation and protection of his wealth.[52] For the many speak of things such as the good producer and custodian of property, but not of philanthropic and sharing tendencies, quite apart from the fact that they know nothing about things on which you cannot place [specific figures].[53] Indeed, it is not easy for such a man to make [much] money starting with little nor, once he makes it, [to keep it.] Thus, this man will perhaps be much the best at measuring what is advantageous to both acquisition and maintenance, so that he does not toil for the sake of possessions more than he enjoys them. For it is clear that neither the pain involved in every kind

ανοῦν κτῆσιν [ἄ]δηλος αὐτῶ[ι
δῆλον ὡς οὔθ' ἡ τέρψις ἡ δι-

COLUMN XIX

ὰ τ[ὴν κτῆσι]ν, οὔτ' ἀμείνων ἄλ-
λος τὴν ὑπεροχὴν αὐτῶν πρὸς
ἄλληλα θεωρῆσαι καὶ μνημο-
νεύειν. Κτᾶσθαι μέντοι γ' οὐ
δυνήσεται πλεῖστα καὶ τάχι-   5
στα καὶ διαθεωρεῖν, ὅθεν ἂν
μάλιστα τὸ πλεῖον αὔξοι[το,
μηδὲν ἀπομετ[ρῶ]ν πρὸς τὸ
τέλος ἀλλὰ πρὸς τὸ πλέον
καὶ τοὔλαττον, καὶ τὰ προϋ-   10
πάρχοντ' ἀεὶ φυλάττειν ἐν-
τόνως· πολὺς γὰρ ὁ πόνος
ἤδη περὶ τοῦτο καὶ μετὰ φρον-
τίδος σκληρᾶς γιγνόμενος
καὶ πᾶν τιθε[ίση]ς ἐν πενίαι   15
τὸ δυσχερές, ἐναργῶς τῆς
φύσεω[ς δει]κνυούσης, ἄν τις
αὐτῆ[ι] προ[σ]έχ[ηι], διότι καὶ τοῖς
ὀλίοις εὐκόλ[ω]ς χρήσεθ', [ὁ] δὲ
πλοῦτος μέτ[ρ]ον τι φροντί-   20
δος κα[ὶ π]όνου πρὸς τὴν δι'
αὐτὸν ἐ[π]ικουρίαν ἀλλα[κ]τὸν
ποιεῖ.* Ἄλλον μὲν οὖν ἐνίο-
τ]ε το[ι]οῦτον ὑπάρχειν ὥσ-
περ [ὑ]πηρέτη[ν] οὐκ ἄχαρι κα-   25
θάπερ καὶ τὸ[ν] ἄκρον περὶ
τὴν τοῦ σίτου κατεργασί-
αν, αὐτὸν δ' ἐρ[γά]την τῶν το[ι-
ούτων οὐκ [ἐπιτ]ήδειον εἶ-
ναι· οὐ [γ]ὰρ ἔτι λ[υ]σιτελεῖ πρὸς   30
τὴν κακοπαθίαν ἀναμετρου-
μένη [κ]τῆσις τ[ο]ιαύτη. Τοιοῦ-
τον οὖν ὄντα τὸν σοφὸν περὶ τὴν ἐπιμέλ[εια]ν καὶ τὴν

whatsoever of acquisition nor the pleasure deriving from [acquisition] are unknown to him,

Column XIX

nor is there any other person better (than he is) at observing and remembering where one of these things (sc. pain or pleasure) exceeds the other. Nonetheless, he will not be able to acquire a very large quantity of possessions and in a very short time. Nor (will he be able) to examine closely in what manner the greater part of his possessions could increase as much as possible, so long as he does not at all measure (it) out with regard to the final goal, but only with regard to "the more and the less." Nor yet (will he be able) to watch always with eagerness over the possessions that he already has. Indeed, the trouble that this latter involves is already much, and it is accompanied by bitter worry [that locates] all adversity in poverty, although nature shows very clearly, if only one [pays attention to her], that she will be easily satisfied with few possessions,[54] while wealth repays a certain measure of care and toil for the purpose of succor. It is not, then, disagreeable that sometimes there should be another person of this kind, in the role of a servant, just like the expert in the production of bread. But that he himself (sc. the true philosopher) should be a producer of such things is inappropriate. For this kind of acquisition, when measured against toil, is no longer profitable.[55] So, given that such is the

φυλακὴν τῶν χρημάτων   35
οὐκ ἐνοχλήσει π[λοῦ]τος ὑ-
πάρχων, οὐδ' ἐφ' ὅσον ἂν ἐνο-
χλῇ, ἐπὶ πλέον τοῦτο ποή-
σει ἢ τὰς χάριτας [ἀ]ποδώσει,
κατά τ[ε τ]ὴν κτῆσιν ὡσαύ-   40
τως τὸ συμφέρον ἀκολου-
θήσει τ[ῷ]ι σοφῶι, χρη-
ματισ[τή]ν τε ἀγαθὸν αὐ[τὸν
οὐθὲν μὲν ἴσως δ[ιο]ίσει π[ρο]σ-
ειπεῖν, ἐπειδὴ κατὰ τὸ συμ-   45
φέρ[ον] μάλιστ[α] καὶ κτᾶται
καὶ χρῆται καὶ ἐπιμέ[λεται

COLUMN XX

πλούτο]υ. Οὐ μὴν [ἀπο]-
βιαστέον²⁶ γε τοῦτ' ἐστιν δ[ιὰ
τῶν κατὰ τὰς ἑρμηνείας συ[ν-
ηθ]ειῶν καὶ ταῦτα μηθὲν ἐν-
δεικνυμένους περὶ τῆς τοῦ   5
σοφοῦ [κ]τήσεώς τε καὶ χρή-
σεως, ὥσπερ οἱ σοφισταὶ ποιοῦσιν, ἀλλ' ἀνάγοντας ἐπὶ τὴν
ὑπάρχουσαν ἡμῖν πρόληψι[ν
περὶ ἀγαθοῦ χρηματ[ιστ]οῦ,   10
σκεπτέον τε ἐν τίνι τὸ προ-
ειλημμένον καὶ τῶι πῶς χρη-
ματιζομένωι, καὶ [ῷι] ἂν ἐκεῖ-
ν' ἐπιμαρτυρῆται, κατηγορη-
τέον τ[ού]του χρηματιστὴν   15
ἀγαθόν· διόπερ εἰ μὲν βου-
λόμεθα λέγειν ἐν προλήψει
τοῦτον ἀγαθὸν χρηματιστὴ[ν
τὸν κα[τὰ] τὸ συμφέρον κτώ-
μενον [κα]ὶ ἐπιμελόμενον   20

---

26. Delattre, Tsouna; ἀλ[όγως | βια[στ]έον Jensen.

wise man with regard to the care and maintenance of his possessions, the [wealth] that he has will not bring him trouble nor, to the extent that it does trouble him, will it do so more than it will render the benefits back to him. And in a similar manner, advantage will follow the wise man with regard to the acquisition of wealth. And perhaps [it will not matter] to call [him] a good moneymaker, since he is the person who acquires, uses, and [takes care of wealth] to the greatest advantage.

COLUMN XX

We must not, on the other hand, [violate] this (sc. the meaning of the expression "the good moneymaker") through [the ordinary usage] of linguistic expressions, as sophists do,[56] especially as we would be showing nothing about the acquisition and use (of wealth) pertaining to the wise man. Rather, we must refer to the preconception that we possess about a good moneymaker, ask in whom the content of that preconception is substantiated and in what manner that person makes money, and ascribe the predicate "good moneymaker" [to whoever it may be in whom] those features are attested. For just this reason, if we want to claim that, in the preconception, the good moneymaker is the one who acquires and takes care of wealth in accordance with what is advantageous, then we must

π[λο]ύτου, τὸν σοφὸν μάλιστα
το[ι]οῦτον εἶναι ῥητέον· εἰ [δὲ
μᾶλλον ἐπὶ τὸν δυνατῶς
καὶ ἐντέχνως πολλὰ πορι-
ζ]ό[μεν]ον καὶ μήτε αἰσχρῶς   25
ἐννόμ[ω]ς τε φέρομεν ἐν
προλήψει τὸν ἀγαθὸν χρη-
ματιστήν, κἂν ὅτι μάλιστα
πλεῖ[ον κα]κοπαθῇ κτώμε-
νος [οὕτω]ς ἤπερ ἤδηται, μᾶλ-   30
λο]ν ἄλλο[υ]ς τῶν σοφῶν φατέ-
ον. Οὐθὲ[ν γ]ὰρ ἀφαιρουμένη
τοῦ σοφ[οῦ] ἡ τοιαύτη κατη-
γο]ρία ····· ειαν μόνον μη-
·· νθ ······ ας ἡ γιγνο[μ]έ-   35
νη κατὰ τὸ [σ]υμφέρον κτή-
σ[ε]ι τε καὶ ο[ἰκ]ονομίαι πλο[ύ-
του. Τῶι γ[ὰ]ρ μὴ ὁρᾶν περὶ
τοῦ ὅπως [π]ρ[οεσ]τῶτας χρημάτων ἀκ[ο]λο[υ]θεῖ τὸ συμ-   40
φέρ]ον ζηλοῦ[μ]εν τοὺς πολ-
λὰ καὶ ταχέως κτωμένους
ἡ[γ]ούμενοι τούτοις ὑπάρ-
χ[ει]ν [τὸν] λυσιτελῆ τῶι βίωι
χρημ[ατ]ισμόν. Οἱ δὲ φιλοσο-   45
φε[ῖν] φάσ[κο]ντες, ἐξὸν λέγειν
ἡμῖν παρ' ἃς αἰτίας ὁ σοφὸς ἐ-
π' ὠ[φελίαι] μάλιστα κ[α]ὶ κτή-

COLUMN XXI

σεται καὶ κυριε[ύσει χρ]ημάτων
καὶ ὅλως ἐμφαίνειν ἡ ποία
βελτίστη διοίκησις, τοῦτο
μὲν οὐ ποιοῦσιν, μόνον δὲ
ἐφαρμόσαι ζητοῦσιν ἐπὶ τὸν   5
σοφὸν τὴν τοιαύτην κατη-
γορίαν καὶ ταῦτ' οὐκ ἐπὶ πρό-
ληψιν ἀνάγοντες, ἣν ἔχο-

proclaim the sage above all as such a man. But if, on the other hand, in the preconception, we apply the quality of the good moneymaker rather to the man [who obtains for himself] many possessions with ability and expertise, and also not in a dishonorable way but lawfully, however much it may be true that [in this mode of acquisition] he encounters more sufferings than pleasures, then we must affirm that it is people other than sages who belong to that category (sc. of good moneymakers). For since that predication does not detract at all from the sage ... only ... that is achieved both by the acquisition and the administration of wealth according to what is advantageous. In truth, by failing to see how those people [whom advantage follows control their money], we envy those who acquire many goods and in a short time, because we believe that these men are pursuing the kind of moneymaking that benefits one's life. Besides, while we can say *for what reasons* the sage will be the person who both acquires and possesses money to the greatest [advantage],

Column XXI

and while we can generally *show* which is the best kind of management, nevertheless those who pretend to be philosophers do not do that but only seek to apply such a predicate to the wise man and, what is more, do so *not* by referring it to the preconception that we have about a good

μεν ὑπὲρ ἀγαθοῦ χρηματι-
στοῦ, ἀλλὰ καὶ κατὰ τὰς τῶν   10
λέξεων ὁμιλίας ἀποβιαζό-
μενοι.* Τὸ παράπαν γὰρ οὔτ' ἐν
τοῖς ἄλλοις ἐοίκασιν ἐθέλειν
κα]τὰ τὸ προει[ρ]ημένον αἰεὶ
τοὺς λόγους ὑπὲρ τῶν ἀ-   15
γνοουμένων ποεῖσθαι οὔ-
τ' ἐπ' αὐτοῦ τοῦ ν[ῦν] ἐνεστῶ-
τ]ος, ἀλλὰ δεινο[ί] εἰ[σι]ν ὑπὸ
τ]ῶν κατὰ τὰς λέξεις συ[ν]η-
θε[ι]ῶν [ἑ]λκυσθῆναι πρὸς [τὰς   20
περὶ τῶν πραγμάτων ἀπο-
φάσεις, κἄπειτα δ[ιδ]άσκειν²⁷
ὡς τούς τε πολλοὺς ἐξελέγ-
χο[ντ]ες ἔνθ' ἂν ἐναντίως
αὐτοῖς] κατηγο[ρ]ῶσιν ὑπὲρ   25
τῶν αὐτῶν, καὶ τῶν ἀγ[νο-
ουμένων τι διδά[σ]κοντες,
ὅ[π]ερ Ἀριστοτέλης ἔπαθεν
κα]τὰ τὸν ἐν τῶι Πε[ρ]ὶ π[λού-
του] λόγον ὑπὲρ τοῦ τὸν [μ]ὲν   30
ἀγα]θὸν ἄνδρα καὶ χρημ[ατι-
σ[τὴ]ν ἀγαθὸν εἶναι, τὸν δ[ὲ
φ[αῦλ]ον καὶ χρηματιστὴν
φαῦ]λον, ὡς ὁ Μητρόδωρος [ἀ-
πέ[δ]ειξεν. Ἐκ δὴ τούτων   35
ἔσ[τιν] διαλαμβά[ν]ειν προα[ι-
ρο[υμ]ένοις καὶ τὸ πόσης κτ[ή-
σεω[ς] ἐπιμελητέον, καὶ τίνα
καὶ [π]οίαν οἰκονομίαν ἐν
τῶι λόγωι λαμβάνομεν, καὶ   40
πῶς οἰκονόμον ἀγαθὸν ἔσ-
τιν εἰπεῖν τὸν σοφὸν καὶ πῶς
οὐκ ἔστιν, ὡσαύτως δὲ καὶ
χρ[η]ματιστήν, καὶ τίς οἰκο-

---

27. Jensen; δ[όξα]ν σχεῖν Delattre.

moneymaker but by actually doing violence (to the preconception) on the basis of conventional ways of talking.[57] For they certainly do not give the impression of wishing always to conduct discussions about the things that they do not know in accordance with the method indicated above,[58] either in other matters or about the issue presently at hand. On the contrary, they are deft at being drawn by the habits of ordinary speech to deny the reality of things, and then at assuming the role of the teacher[59] as if they were refuting the many wherever the many apply predicates to the same things in a manner opposite [to their own], teaching something they do not know. In fact, as Metrodorus has shown, this is what happened to Aristotle in the course of the argument developed in the treatise [*On Wealth*] regarding the thesis that the [good] man is also a good moneymaker, whereas the [bad] one is also a [bad] moneymaker. From these (sc. Metrodorus's) arguments it becomes possible for those who wish it to understand how many possessions we should take care of; which and what kind of property management we assume in our discussion; in what sense we can call the wise man a good property manager—and likewise moneymaker—and in what sense we cannot; which type of property man-

νομ[ί]α τέχνη καὶ τ[ίς οὐ   45
τ[έχνη] δυναμένη δὲ [καθά-
πε[ρ ὑπ]ὸ πολλ[ῶ]ν οὕτω καὶ ὑ-
πὸ [τοῦ] σοφο[ῦ γ]ίνεσθαι, καὶ δι-

Column XXII

ὅτι σ[υμφέρουσα] καὶ λυσιτελὴ[ς
ἡ τοι[αύτη] πρὸς ἄκραν εὐετηρίαν ἐκείνη δὲ ἀλυσιτελὴς
καὶ ταλαίπωρος, καὶ πῶς δι-
ακείμενον χρὴ ποιεῖσθαι τὰ[ς   5
ἐπιμελείας. Ἔστιν δ᾽ ἀνελέ-
σθαι τι[νὰ] καὶ πρὸς τὸ πόθεν
καὶ πῶς πορίζεσθαι δεῖ καὶ
φυλάττειν. Ἡ συνέχουσα μέντοι γ᾽ ἀνάτασις αὐτῶι γέγο-   10
νεν πρὸς τὸ μακρῶι μᾶλλον
λυσιτελεῖν τὰς ποτε γινο-
μένας ὀχλήσεις καὶ φροντί-
δας καὶ πραγματείας τῆς
ἐναντίας αἱρέ[σ]εως εἰς   15
διαγωγὴν τὴν ἀρίστην.
Ἡμε[ῖς] δὲ [λ]έγωμεν ἀκολουθοῦντες [τὸ] μὲν ο[ἴεσ]θαι
πορισμὸν ἄ[ριστο]ν εἶναι τὸν
δορίκτητον κα[ὶ χ]ρῆσιν οἵ-   20
αν ἐποήσατο Γ[ε]λλίας ὁ Σι-
κελιώτης καὶ Σκόπας ὁ Θετ-
ταλὸς καὶ Κίμων καὶ Νικίας
οἱ Ἀθηναῖοι δοξοκόπων ἀνθρώπων εἶναι κατὰ σοφίαν οὐδε-   25
τέραν, ὡς κᾶν [α]ὐτοὶ μαρτυ-
ρήσειεν οἱ βίοι τῶν τὰ τοιαῦτα γραφόντων· ὅλως [δ]ὲ φαί-
νονται τὰ[ς ἐπι]τ[εύ]ξεις {ἐοι-
κόσιν} εἰς τοὺς πο[λ]ιτικοὺς ἀ-   30
νατιθέναι καὶ τ[οὺ]ς πρακτι-
κούς, ὥστε πολλ[ά]κις [ἂν ἐ]πε-

agement is an art and [which is not an art] but can be practiced by [the] sage, [as it can by many people];

Column XXII

why the latter kind of administration is [useful] and advantageous for faring best, whereas the former is disadvantageous and troublesome; and, finally, in which state of mind one ought to engage in these activities. One can also take up some points about the questions from what sources and in what manner one should obtain and watch over one's possessions. However, his (sc. Metrodorus's) continuous effort has been to establish that the occasional disturbances, cares, and labors are far more useful in the long run for the best way of life than the opposite choice. Let us follow him and declare that [to believe] that the [best] way to acquire goods is to win them by the spear and the best use of them the kind made by Gellias of Sicily, Scopas of Thessaly, and the Athenians Cimon and Nicias,[60] is characteristic of vainglorious men and in accordance with neither kind of wisdom (sc. neither practical nor contemplative), as the very *Lives* of those authors who write such things would testify.[61] Indeed, they[62] generally appear to attribute these [achievements] to the politicians and the

ρωτῆσα[ι τί]να ποτὲ πε-
ρίεστιν τοῖς σ[χολά]ζουσι πε-
ρὶ τὴν ἀλήθειαν [καὶ πά]ντα ταῦ-   35
τ’ ἐπικρίν[ο]υσιν· ο[ὐ γὰ]ρ ἐοίκασιν οἱ αὐτοὶ κατά γ[ε το]ύτους
ἐργάται τ[ε] εἶναι τῶν καλῶν,
ὅσα πρὸς [τ]ὴν ἐκ τῶν κ[υ]ριω-
τάτων ἀταραξία[ν σ]υντείν[ει,   40
καὶ θεωρ[η]ταί, ἀλλ’ ἢ μ[ὴ] ἔ[χ]ειν
τὸ τέλος τοῦτ’ ἐπιφέρουσαν
ἀρετ[ὴ]ν φ[ή]σουσι δῆλον ὅτ[ι
τοὺς περὶ τὴν ἀλήθει[α]ν δει-
νούς, ἢ μηδὲν ἀπ’ αὐτῆς [ἀξι-   45
όλογον [συ]ντελεῖσθαι, [ἢ πόλεως ἢ δυνάμεως ἡγουμέ[ν]ω[ν
τῶν ἐν σ[ο]φίαι περιττῶν [γενή-

Column XXIII

σεσθαι πεῖρα]ν. Γελοι[ότατον
δὲ καὶ τὸ πορίζειν ἀφ’ ἱππικ[ῆς
καλὸν οἴεσθαι, τὸ δ’ ‘ἀπὸ με[ταλ-
λικῆς, δούλων ἐρ[γ]αζομέν[ων’
οὐκ εὔκληρον, τὸ δ’ ‘ἐξ ἀμφο-   5
τέρων, αὐτὸν ἐνεργοῦντα’
μανικόν· ταλαίπωρον δὲ καὶ
τὸ ‘γεωργο[ῦν]τ’ αὐτὸν οὕτως
ὥστε αὐτουργεῖν’· τὸ δ’ ‘ἄλλων,
ἔχοντα γῆν’ κατὰ σπουδαῖ-   10
ον· ἥκιστα γὰρ ἐπιπλοκὰς ἔ-
χει πρὸς ἀνθρώπους, ἐξ ὧν
ἀηδίαι πολλαὶ παρακολου-
θοῦσι, καὶ διαγωγὴν ἐπιτερπῆ καὶ μετὰ φίλων ἀναχώρη-   15
σιν εὔσχολον καὶ παρὰ τοῖς
σώφροσι]ν εὐσχημονεστά-
την πρόσοδον. Ο[ὐκ ἄ]σχ[η-
μον [δ’ ο]ὐδὲ ἀπὸ συνοικία[ς τε
καὶ δούλων ἐμπειρίας ἢ καὶ   20

men of action, so that one could often ask what in the world is left for those who [devote themselves to study] concerning the truth and who consider all these issues. For, at least according to them, the people who do all the noble deeds that contribute to the tranquillity that derives from the most important things (sc. politicians and military men) and those who contemplate (the truth) are not the same people, but obviously they will claim either that the ones who are wonderfully gifted regarding the search for truth [do not have] the excellence that achieves this aim (sc. tranquillity), or that nothing remarkable is accomplished because of it, [or that] if a city or army were led by those who excel in wisdom. ...

Column XXIII

... It is [utterly] ridiculous to believe that it is a good thing to earn an income from practicing the art of horsemanship.[63] Earning an income "from the art of mining with slaves doing the labor" is unfortunate, and as to securing income "from both these sources by means of one's own labor," it is a mad thing to do.[64] "Cultivating the land oneself in a manner involving work with one's own hands" is also wretched, while (cultivating it) "using other workers if one is a landowner" is appropriate for the good man.[65] For it brings the least possible involvement with men from whom many disagreeable things follow, and a pleasant life, a leisurely retreat with one's friends, and a most dignified income to [those who are moderate]. Nor is it disgraceful to earn an income both from properties rented to tenants and from slaves who have skills or even arts that are in no way

τέχνας ἐχόντων μηδαμ[ῶς
ἀπρεπεῖς. Ἀλλὰ ταῦτα δεύ-
τερα καὶ τρίτα· πρῶτον δὲ
καὶ κάλλιστον ἀπὸ λόγων
φιλο[σό]φων ἀνδράσιν δεκτι-   25
κοῖς μεταδιδομέν[ων] ἀν-
τιμεταλαμβάνειν εὐχάρι-
στο[ν ἅμ]α μετὰ σεβασμοῦ
παντ[ός], ὡς ἐγένετ' Ἐπικο[ύ-
ρωι, λο[ιπὸ]ν δὲ ἀληθινῶν καὶ   30
ἀφιλο[ν]ε[ί]κων καὶ [σ]υ[λ]λήβδη[ν
εἰπεῖν [ἀτ]αράχων, ὡς τό γε δι-
ὰ σοφ[ιστι]κῶν καὶ ἀγωνιστι-
κ]ῶν ο[ὐδέν] ἐστι βέλτιον τοῦ
διὰ δη[μοκ]οπικῶν καὶ συκο-   35
φαντικ[ῶν]. Ὧν δ' ἐπιτηδευ-
τέον εἰς π[ρ]όσοδον καὶ τήρη-
σιν ταύτης τε καὶ τῶν προϋ-
παρχόν[τ]ων τὸ μὲν συνέ-
χ]ον ἡγητέον ἐν τῆι τῶν ἐ-   40
πιθυμιῶν εὐσταλείαι καὶ τῶν
φ]όβων· οὐ[δ]ὲν γὰρ ἐχεῖν
κ]α[ὶ ἀ]νατρέπειν εἴ[θιστ]αι λαμ-
προτάτα[ς καὶ πλ]ουσι[ωτάτας
οἰκίας ὡ]ς πολυτέλι[αί τε] δι-   45
αίτ]ης κα[ὶ] λαγνε[ῖαι καὶ] π[ε-

Column XXIV

ριβλέψε[ις] κα[ὶ γυν]α[ικ]ισμοὶ
καὶ τὰ τούτοις ὁμοιό[τ]ροπα,
καὶ πάλ[ι]ν ἐκστατ[ι]κὴ φρίκη θε-
ῶν καὶ θανάτου καὶ [ἀλ]γηδό-
νων καὶ τῶν ταῦτα παρασκε[υ-   5
άζειν δοξαζομένων, ὥστε
ἂν ζῆλον ἀζήλων καὶ φόβον
ἀφόβων ἐφ' ὅ<σο>ν ἐνδέχεται
περιαιρῇ τις αὑτοῦ, καὶ πορι-
στικὸς ἔσται καὶ φυλακτικὸς   10

unseemly. However, these sources of income come second and third. The first and noblest thing is to receive back thankful gifts with all reverence in return for philosophical discourses shared with men capable of understanding them, as happened to Epicurus,[66] and, [moreover], discourses that are truthful and free of strife and, [in short], serene, since in fact the acquisition of an income* through [sophistical] and contentious speeches is [in no way] better than its acquisition through demagogical and slandering ones.[67] Of the recommended activities leading to profits and the maintenance both of these and of the possessions that one had beforehand, one must keep in mind that the principal one consists in managing one's desires and fears.[68] For, [usually], nothing drains and ruins the most illustrious and [richest houses] so much as [extravagance in lifestyle], lechery, ostentatious actions,

COLUMN XXIV

[effeminate behavior], and similar things and, again, the chilling fear of the gods, of death, of pains and of the things that are believed to produce them. Consequently, if one removes from oneself, to the extent that it is possible, the envy of things that are not to be envied and the fear of things that are not to be feared, one will be able both to procure and to preserve (one's property) in the appropriate manner. Injustice too is thought to

* Cf. τὸ πορίζειν: XXIII.2.

ὡς προσῆκε<ι>. Καὶ ἀδικία δὲ
νομίζεται μὲν ἑκάτερον
ποιεῖν, στερίσκει δ᾽ [ἔπ]ειτα τὸ
πλεῖστον οὐ μόνον τῶν
κ[ερ]δανθέντων ἀλλὰ καὶ   15
τῶν προϋπαρχόντων, ὥσ-
τε ἂν καὶ δικαιοσύνην ἀσκῆι,
τὸ γ᾽ ἐπὶ ταύ[τ]ην [ἀ]κινδύνως
καὶ ποριεῖ καὶ φ[υλ]άξει. Καὶ
μὴν ἀφιλία δοκεῖ μὲν ἀνα-   20
λωμάτων κουφίζε[ιν], ἀσυν-
εργήτους δὲ ποιεῖ καὶ ὑπὸ
παντὸς καταφρονουμένους καὶ
ὑ]π᾽ εὐνοίας ἀπολυωρήτους,
ἐξ ὧν οὔτε πρόσοδος ἀξι-   25
όλογος οὔτε τήρ[η]σις ἀσφα-
λής, ὥστε ἂν φιλίαν περιποι-
ῆ]ται, καθ᾽ ἑκάτε[ρον] εὐτυχή-
σ]ει. Καὶ ἀφιλανθ[ρω]πία δὲ
κ]αὶ ἀνημερότης ζημιοῖ πολ-   30
λ]ὰ καὶ ἀβοη[θ]ήτου[ς] ποιεῖ, πολ-
λ]άκις δ᾽ ἄρδ[η]ν ἀν[αρ]πάζεσθαι
τ]ὴν οὐσίαν. [Α]ἱ δ᾽ ἐν[α]ντίαι δι-
α]θέσεις τἀναν[τί]α [παρα]σκευ-
ά]ζουσιν, οἶμαι δὲ [καὶ] πᾶσαν   35
ἁ]πλῶς κακίαν ἐνπο[δί]ζειν
πρὸς ἐπιτερπῆ συν[αγ]ωγὴν
κα]ὶ τῶν ὑπαρχόντ[ων] ἐπιμέ-
λειαν, τὰς δ᾽ ἀντικε[ιμ]ένας
ἀρετὰς συνεργεῖν ἀξ[ιο]λόγως.   40
Ὡς δ᾽ ἰδιώτερον εἰπεῖν, αἱ
φίλοις καὶ τῶν ἄλλων τοῖς οὐ-
κ ἀτόποις γινόμεναι μετα-
δόσεις ἀφαιρέσεις [κ]αὶ τῆς
ὑπάρξεω[ς] με[ιώ]σεις ἐνίοις   45
εἶναι δο[κο]ῦ[σιν], εἰσὶν δὲ
κτήσει[ς λ]υσιτελέστεραι

bring about each one of these things (sc. the acquisition and preservation of property), but, in fact, afterwards it takes away the greatest part not only of what one has gained but also of what one has had beforehand. It follows that, if one actually practices justice, one will both obtain and safeguard the gain acquired in conformity with it.[69] Further, while the lack of friends seems to relieve one's expenses, in fact it causes people to remain without support, to be held in contempt by everybody, and to be little honored by the favors of benefactors. On account of these features, neither is one's income considerable nor is its preservation secure, so that it is if one acquires friends that one will be happy in both these respects.[70] Moreover, lack of human feeling and harshness do much damage and leave men helpless and often cause their property to be utterly ravaged, whereas the contrary dispositions bring about contrary effects. Indeed, I believe that absolutely every vice raises obstacles to the pleasant collection and to the maintenance of one's possessions, whereas their opposite virtues contribute considerably to them. To speak more precisely, acts of imparting money to one's friends and, of one's other acquaintances, to those free of wickedness [seem] to some people to amount to subtractions from and diminutions of the property. But in fact,

Column XXV

κα[τὰ] τὸν Ἕρμαρχον ἐπιμέλει-
αι τ[ο]ιούτων ἀνδρῶν ἤπερ
ἀγρῶν καὶ πρὸς τὴν τύχην
ἀσφαλέστατοι θησαυροί. Δεῖ
δὲ τὸν μέλλοντα καὶ συνάξειν   5
τι καὶ τὸ συναχθὲν φυλάξειν
μὴ²⁸ 'τὸ παρὸν εὖ ποιεῖν', κατ' Ἐ-
πίχαρμον, οὐ μόνον δαπά-
νης ἀλλὰ καὶ τοῦ προφανέν-
τος κέρδους ἁρπαστικὸν   10
γινόμενον, προνοεῖν δὲ καὶ
τοῦ μέλλοντος· καὶ γὰρ νῦν
εὐέλπιδας ποιεῖ καὶ παρὸν
γινόμενον εὐφρ[αί]νει· καὶ
μὴ μόνον τοῦτο ποιεῖν,   15
ἀλλὰ καὶ τῶν ἰδίων προΐε-
σθαί τι πολλάκ[ις], ὥ[σ]περ οἱ
τὴν γῆν σπείροντες, ἐξ ὧν
πρα[γμ]άτων (περὶ γὰ[ρ ἀ]νθρώ-
πων ε[ἴ]παμεν) πολλαπ[λάσι-   20
α καρπίζεσθαι γίνεται, [φ]ειδομένοις
δ' ὀλίγον ὑπεριδεῖν οὐ γίνε-
ται· καὶ κατὰ τὰς ὑπάρξεις ἀ-
ναλίσκε[ι]ν, μὴ τῶι πολλοῦ καὶ
ὀλίγου νομίσματ[ο]ς ὠνεῖ-   25
σθαι [χ]ανονίζοντ[α]ς· ὃ γ[ὰ]ρ
τῶιδε τίμιον τῶιδ' [εὔ]ων[ον,
καὶ ὃ [τῶ]ιδε μεμπτὸν πρί[α-
σθαι [τῶ]ι ταχὺ συνελε[ῖ]ν [τὴ]ν
ὕπαρξ[ι]ν, ἐὰν συνεχίζῃ, τ[ῶι-   30
δε ἄ[μεμ]πτον. Ἄτο[πο]ν δ', [ὥ]ς
προεί[πα]μεν, καὶ τὸ διατ[άτ-
τεσθα[ι] κατὰ μῆνα καὶ κα[τά-

---

28. The negative μή should be left out of the quotation.

COLUMN XXV

according to Hermarchus, the cares bestowed upon such men represent more profitable acquisitions than lands, and they are the safest treasures with regard to the turns of fortune. Indeed, the person who is going to gather together some possessions and to preserve what he has collected should not "take advantage of the present," as Epicharmus recommends,[71] becoming eager to snatch up not only the money that he needs to spend but also any gain that may leap to the eye, but, on the contrary, he should provide, precisely, for the future. For this strategy both gives us good hopes right now and, when it comes to be present, makes us happy. And not only should he do this, but also he should often give away part of his own possessions, just like those who sow seeds in the earth. From these things—for we have been speaking about human beings—it becomes possible to reap many times more fruits, whereas this does not happen to people who refrain from discounting a small part of their income. Further, people should spend money in proportion to their income and not determine their expenses according to the high or low price of things (sc. their market price). For what is costly for one man is [cheap] for another, and the thing whose purchase brings blame upon one man because, if (this kind of purchase) continues, it destroys his property, nonetheless it [does not bring any blame upon another].[72] And, as we said before, it is equally absurd to make arrangements month by month regarding the

γειν²⁹ [κα]τ' ἔτος ἴσον ἑκά[στοτ]ε,
ἀνάγ[κης γ]ινομένης ἔστι[ν   35
ὅτε πο[λλ]ῶι πλέον δαπαν[ᾶν,
καὶ τὸ τ[ῶν] προσγινομένων,
ὥς γ' ἔνι[ο]ι Ῥωμαίων ποιοῦσιν, τὸ μ[ὲ]ν εἰς δαπάνην, τὸ
δ' εἰς κα[τ]ασκευήν, τ[ὸ] δ' εἰ[ς ἀ-   40
ναπλήρωσιν, τὸ δ' ε[ἰς] θησαυ-
ρισμὸν μερίζειν, ὥσ[πε]ρ οὐ-
χὶ τῶν καιρῶν ἀναγ[κ]αζόν-
των καὶ τῆς καλοκἀ[γ]αθίας
ἐνίοτε μήτε κατα[σ]κευά-   45
ζ]ειν μήτε θησαυρ[ίζ]ειν ἀλ-
λὰ παραμετρεῖν τ[οῖ]ς πρά-
γ[μ]ασιν καὶ ταῖς ἡδε[ί]αις ἐπι-

Column XXVI

φοραῖς.* Χρὴ δὲ, καθάπερ πλειόνων προσπεσόντων χαρίζε-
σθαι ταῖς ἀβλαβέσι τῶν ὀρέ-
ξεων αὐτοῖς καὶ φίλοις, οὕτω
συμβάσης ἁδρᾶς κοιλότητος   5
ἀναμάχεσθαι ταῖς μὴ ἀνελευ-
θέροις συστολαῖς, καὶ μᾶλλόν
γε ταῖς εἰς αὑτοὺς ἢ ταῖς εἰς
φίλους, καὶ πρὸς ἐπισκέψεις
καὶ παρεδρείας ἐνίοις καὶ   10
συλλογισμῶν συνθέσεις
κατατίθεσθαί τινας χρόνους
μήτε αἰσχύ[ν]εσθαι μήτε
φιλοσοφίας δοκεῖν ἀφαιρεῖν·
τὸ γὰρ πλεονάζον αἰσχρόν   15
ἐστιν, ἀλλ' ἐφ' ὅσον χρήσιμον,
εὔσχημον, αἰσχρὸν δὲ πά-
λιν τὸ μηδ[ὲ] ἕν· καὶ περὶ τὰς

---

29. Jensen; κα[ταρ]-|γεῖν Delattre.

disposition of one's goods and [to restore][73] each time the same quantity
of goods year by year,[74] since sometimes [it becomes necessary] to spend
much more. And it is equally absurd to divide up the income from additional resources, just as [some] Romans do, so that one part of it is for
expenses, another is for furnishings, another for restoration, yet another
for savings, as if circumstances and the sense of decorum did not force
one sometimes neither to buy furnishings nor to save, but to measure (the
expenses) against the circumstances and the pleasure of offering things.

COLUMN XXVI

Now, as one ought to indulge oneself and one's friends in those desires
that are harmless when a larger quantity of goods has happened to come
to hand, so, when there has been serious shortage of cash, one ought to
compensate for the losses with retrenchements that are not illiberal and
that are applied more toward oneself than toward one's friends.[75] Moreover, one ought to dedicate some time to inspections, to giving assistance
to some (workers), and to preparing one's accounts, without either feeling
shame or believing that (by acting in that manner) one takes something
away from philosophy. For while it is a shameful thing to be excessively
involved in such matters, to the extent that this is useful it is honorable,
and the shameful thing is rather to do nothing at all. Further, regarding

ἐγλογὰς τ[ῶ]ν ἐπιτηδείων
ἐπιτρόπων τε καὶ ὑποτετα-   20
γμένων καὶ κτημάτων καὶ
συναλλαγμάτων καὶ παν-
τὸς τοῦ πρὸς οἰκονομία[ν
μὴ μονογνωμονεῖν, ἀ[λ]λ[ὰ
συνπαραλαμβάνειν καὶ φί-   25
λους τοὺς μ[ά]λιστ᾽ εὐθέτους
καὶ τοὺς καθ᾽ ἕκαστον ἐμ-
πείρου[ς. Κ]α[ὶ πε]ρ[ὶ] οἰκε[τῶν] κτῆ-
σίν τε καὶ χρ[ῆσ]ιν ἐπιτήδ[ει-
ον εἰς προσό[δο]υς καὶ τηρ[ή-   30
σεις ἐκ τῆς πε[ρ]ὶ οἰκετῶν [δι]-
αλ[έξ]εως³⁰ ἐξέ[στ]αι μετα[φέ-
ρειν, τὸ δ᾽ ἐντα[ῦ]θα προσκα[ρ-
τερεῖν οὐ[κ] ἀ[να]γκαῖον. Δο-
κοῦσιν δὲ αἱ π[οι]κίλαι κτ[ήσεις   35
τῶν μονοειδ[ῶ]ν ἧτ[τον οὐδ᾽ ὁ-
μαλῶς διαψεύ[δε]ιν, ἐκείν[ων
ἔστιν ὅτε ποιο[υσ]ῶν ἐσχάτ[ως
ἀπορεῖν· καὶ το[ῦ γ᾽] ἀπὸ κτήσ[ε-
ως ὁ λεγόμεν[ο]ς ἐπιρρεῖ[ν   40
πλοῦτος οὐκ εἶναι χείρων
ἀλλ᾽ ἀσφαλέστερος ἐ[νί]οτε
καὶ μετ᾽ εὐελπι[στ]ίας. Ὅτι
δ᾽ οὐ δεῖ πειθομέν[ο]υς ἐνίων
ἐπαγγελίαις ἀμελεῖν ὧν αὐ-   45
τός τις δύναται πορίζειν
ἢ φυλάττειν μηδ᾽ ἀναπλ[ά]τ-

COLUMN XXVII

τοντα κενὰ καὶ κατελ[πίζον-
τα δαπανᾶν ὑγρότερ[ον, δοκεῖ μὲν οὐ δυσχερὲς ε[ἶναι λέγειν, πάσχουσι δ᾽ αὐτὰ [κ]αὶ τῶν

---

30. Delattre, Tsouna; [δι-|αλ[ήψ]εως Jensen.

the choice both of capable bailiffs and of subordinates, of acquisitions, of transactions, and of everything that has to do with the management of the property, one must not be opinionated but call in for advice one's friends as well, especially those who are most suitable and most experienced in each matter. [As to what concerns] the acquisition of slaves and their appropriate [use] for the purpose of increasing and maintaining the property, it will be possible to borrow ideas from [the conversation][76] concerning slaves, and here it will not be necessary to insist on this topic. Next, it seems that [possessions] of different kinds deceive us in our expectations [less than], and not as regularly as, those of one kind, because the latter sometimes reduce us to utter poverty. Also, it seems that the so-called liquid assets are not inferior to the possession of real estate, but rather they are sometimes safer from risk and accompanied by good hopes.[77] Besides, that one should not neglect the goods that one can oneself procure or preserve under the influence of offers of some people, and that one should not spend more freely

COLUMN XXVII

in pursuit of vain images and hopes, these things are not difficult to say. However, many people suffer from them, even philosophers. Thus, if one

φιλοσόφων πολλοί.* Φίλων 5
μὲν τοίνυν ὑπαρχό[ν]των
φειστέον μᾶλλον, ἵν' ἔχωσιν
καὶ τελευτήσαντος ἐ[φ]ό[διον,
καὶ οἷα τ[έ]κνα θετέον, οὐχ ὑ-
παρχόντων δὲ καὶ τῆ[ς ἀ]κ[ρ]ι- 10
βεστέρας οἰκονομίας [ἀ]νε[τέ-
ον, οὐχ ὅτι τ[ῆ]ς φειδοῦς. [Ε]ἰ δέ
τινα καὶ τῶν παρὰ Ξεν[ο]φῶν-
τι καὶ Θεοφράστωι συν[ε]χω-
ροῦμεν οὐκ ἀδόκιμα κ[αὶ] φι- 15
λοσόφοις εἶναι, προσποιητέ-
ον κἀκεῖνα, μᾶλ[λον] αἰσχυνο-
μέ]νους εἴ τι πἀ[ραπ]έμπομεν
ὠφέλιμον ἤτ[οι] μεταφέ-
ρομεν παρ' ἄλλων. Εἰ δὴ κα- 20
ταμέμψεταί τις ἡμῶν πε-
ρὶ οἰκονομίας ἀναγρ[α]φ[όν-
των, ἡμῖν μὲν ἱκανὸς με-
τ' Ἐπικούρου Μητρόδωρος
ἐπιστέλλων καὶ παραινῶν 25
καὶ διοικῶν ἐπ[ι]μελέστερον
καὶ μέχρι μικροτέρων καὶ ποιῶν αὐτός, εἰ καὶ μὴ τὸ πρᾶγμ[α
κ]ατήπειγεν ὡς [φα]ίνεται·
τοὺς δ' ἀπ' ἄλλης ἀγωγῆς ἀ- 30
ναστελλέτωσαν οἱ καὶ σα-
τρ]απικώτεροι τ[ῶν φ]ιλοσό-
φω]ν, οὓς ἀπεθε[ωρή]σαμεν
τὰ] τοιαῦτα λόγου [π]ολλοῦ
κατηξ̣]ιω[κ]ότ[ας]· ἀ[λλ]ὰ δὴ καὶ 35
πι]θανώτερος ἂν [εἶ]ναι δό-
ξ[ει]εν ὁ παντελῶ[ς ὀ]λίγα φή-
σ[ων] ἡμᾶς περὶ πρά[γ]ματος
μ[ε]ιζόνως ὠφελή[σ]οντος·
ἀλλ'] οὐδ' αὐτὸν φοβ[η]σόμε- 40
θ[α] τὸ μὴ πλείονος τερθρεί-
ας δε[ῖ]σθαι τὴν ἀτάραχον οἰκονομίαν καὶ τὸ μ[ικ]ρὰν εἶ-

has friends, one should save more in order that they may have [means of maintaining themselves] even after one's death, and one should regard them as one's children.[78] On the other hand, if one does not have friends, [one should relax] not only the practice of saving money but also the more parsimonious management of property. Now, if we have conceded that, in addition, some of the tenets held by Xenophon and by Theophrastus are not unconvincing even for philosophers, then we shall have to include them too in our survey, for we would feel [more] ashamed if we omit something useful than if we borrow it from others. At this stage, if somebody will accuse us of writing treatises on property management, Metrodorus with the aid of Epicurus will suffice to prove our point, since he gave instructions, exhorted, and administered (the property) with greater diligence and down to more minute details (than we do), and since he practiced (these precepts) himself even if, as it seems, the matter was not very pressing (for him).[79] As to those who approach the issue coming from a different school of thought, let them be held in check by the most stately of philosophers, whom we observed [to have given much attention] to such things. On the other hand, the critic who [will complain] that we say very little about a subject of greater usefulness would seem to have a more plausible case. [Nonetheless], we shall not be intimidated even by him, because we believe that the tranquil administration of one's property

ναι τὴν πλούτου πρὸς πε-
νίαν ὑπεροχὴν ἐν[ν]οοῦν-   45
τες, ἅμα δ᾽ οὐδὲ δυνατοῦ κα-
θεστῶτος ὁρίζειν παρα-
γραφαῖς τὰς ἐπιμελείας, ἀλ-
λ᾽ ὁλοσχερεστέρων ἀνάγ-
                                                                       20

Column XXVIII

κην εἶναι ποιεῖ[σθ]α[ι τ]ὰ̣[ς π]αρ[α-
δόσεις καὶ πολλὰ κατὰ [μέρος]³¹
διεξόδο[ις πρὸς ἐπι-
μέλειαν καὶ φυλακὴν [χρη]μά-
των, καὶ [μ]άλι[στ᾽ ἐ̣]ν τῆ̣[ι περ]ὶ   5
πλούτου καὶ πενίας κα[ὶ τῆι
πε[ρ]ὶ δι[αί]της πολυτε[λοῦς
τε καὶ λ[ι]τῆς καὶ τῆι περ[ὶ
αἱρέσεων καὶ φυγῶν κᾂν εἴ
τινές εἰσιν ἄλλαι τοια[ῦ]ται.   10

---

31. 2 κατὰ [μέρος] Delattre, Tsouna; 2–3 κᾱ̣ν ἅ[λλαις ὑ-|πογράφ[ε]ιν
Jensen.

does not require greater subtlety and that wealth is [only slightly] superior to poverty. At the same time, we believe that, although it is not even possible to mark off the pursuits (of the good property manager) within the limits of a summary,

COLUMN XXVIII

it is, nevertheless, necessary [to hand down a tradition] of the most general principles and to outline [many details][80] in the treatises [concerning] the care and preservation of possessions, and [chiefly in] the treatise on wealth and poverty, the one on the luxurious and the frugal ways of life, the one on things to be chosen and to be avoided, and in any other treatises of this sort.

NOTES

1. The text of column A is heavily restored on the basis of close parallels with the first book of Pseudo-Aristotle, *Oeconomica* (in particular 1344b26–1345a2), which Philodemus attributes to Theophrastus. Henceforth I shall refer to this as Theophrastus's *Oeconomica*, without prejudice as to the question of who its real author is. It is probable that, in the lost part of the text, Philodemus paraphrased Theophrastus, *Oeconomica* 1344b26–1345a2: Theophrastus emphasizes the importance of preserving what one has acquired, for otherwise the acquisition of goods resembles pouring wine into the proverbial winejar with a hole in the bottom; likewise, Philodemus gives priority to the preservation (φυλακή, τὸ φυλάττειν) of possessions in respect of their acquisition (κτῆσις, τὸ κτᾶσθαι, κτητικόν), arrangement (τὸ κοσμητικόν), and use (χρῆσις,τὸ χρηστικόν). A.1–6 corresponds to *Oeconomica* 1344b26–28. But while for Theophrastus arrangement and use are the ends to which acquisition and preservation are the means, for Philodemus all four activities are means to a carefree and pleasurable life. A.6–18 refers to *Oeconomica* 1344b28–34, while A.18–27 corresponds roughly to *Oeconomica* 1344b35–1345a5. In general, column A selectively paraphrases Theophrastus's text in a fairly accurate and unexceptional manner.

2. The reference to the Persian and Spartan methods of preserving one's property especially concerns a feature common to both: the master and the mistress of the household should give personal supervision each to his or her own domain of the household work. Theophrastus suggests that this is characteristic of the Libyan method as well (*Oeconomica* 1345a4–6). A sixth-century B.C.E. cup in the Laconian style shows king Arkesilas of Cyrene personally supervising the loading of a ship, probably with wool (see Hopper 1979, 40 and pl. 21).

3. Philodemus takes Theophrastus's remark that "for small estates the Attic method of disposing of the produce is useful" (1345a18–19) to mean that "the Athenians purchase at the same time as they sell" (1344b33–34). On balance, it would seem that Philodemus's explanation points to exchange mediated by money: selling in order to buy and buying in order to sell, one commodity being exchanged for money and money used in turn to purchase another commodity.

4. Another feature often considered common to the Persian and the Spartan methods of *oikonomia*, the management of the *oikos*, the household, and generally of one's property, is the orderly arrangement of possessions (τετάχθαι, 1344b35) and their keeping them ready for use (εὐχρηστία, 1345b1). "The Spartan method dictates that implements be ready for use. Each should occupy its own place, for in this way it will be handy and will not require seeking out" (1345b1–4).

5. According to Theophrastus, Dion attributed to Dionysius the practice of personally undertaking the arrangement and supervision of everything in his household (1344b35–36).

6. B.5–7 reflects *Oeconomica* 1345a15–16 with one important difference, namely, that Theophrastus and Philodemus, respectively, use the phrase "neither by night nor by day" (μήτε νυκτὸς μήτε ἡμέρας) in connection with different claims. Theophrastus's text runs as follows: καὶ μηδέποτε ἀφύλακτον οἰκίαν εἶναι, ὥσπερ πόλιν, ὅσα τε δεῖ ποιεῖν μήτε νυκτὸς μήτε ἡμέρας παριέναι ("The master and mistress should never leave the house unguarded, as a city is never left unguarded, and they should never, either by night or by day, postpone whatever tasks ought to be done"). Philodemus omits this last precept and as the text is supplemented, he writes: καὶ μηδέποτ[ε ὅλην οἰκίαν ἀφύ]λακτον ε[ἶναι, ὥσπερ πόλιν], μήτε νυκτὸς [μήτε ἡμέρας, ε]ἰωθέναι τε δι[ανίστασθαι ν]ύκτωρ (B.4–8) ("And the house should] never [be left completely] unguarded, [just as a city should not] either during the night [or during the day], and it should be customary [to rise] during the night"). Philodemus then uses the phrase "neither by night nor by day" to emphasize that the house must be guarded at all times, whereas Theophrastus uses it to emphasize the importance of fulfilling one's tasks promptly and without procrastination. Either Philodemus's eye skipped a line or he has a different text or, most likely in my view, he paraphrases Theophrastus in a way that suits his polemical purposes. While he would not object, at least in principle, to Theophrastus's recommendation that one should not postpone what must be done, he denies that the master should personally attend to the safety of the house and never relax about it.

7. This complex claim rests on normative assumptions that Philodemus will later question. On the one hand, the idea that οἰκονομία (property management) as an expert activity benefits from the master's arduous involvement with the οἶκος (the household) has some plausibility. On the other hand, the contention that short and interrupted nights of sleep contribute to health, let alone to philosophy, seems wildly implausible. However, both Theophrastus and Xenophon appear to associate such exercise with physical and mental fitness—a theme that harks back to Socrates and his associates.

8. Neither Theophrastus nor Philodemus, who is simply paraphrasing Theophrastus here, explains why the Attic method is advantageous for small estates but not for larger ones.

9. I.2–8 roughly corresponds to Xenophon, *Oeconomicus* (henceforth *Oec.*) 1.2–3. However, Philodemus's surviving text does not mention Socrates' initial question, whether property management is a discipline (ἐπιστήμη) or an art (τέχνη), and if it is a discipline or an art, what its function (ἔργον) is (*Oec.* 1.1–2). In fact, it is in response to this question that Critoboulos introduces both the notion and a definition of the good property manager (ἀγαθὸς οἰκονόμος) as someone whose characteristic is to manage his own estate well (εὖ οἰκεῖν, 1.2). In I.8–10 Philodemus appears to paraphrase *Oec.* 1.9 using Epicurean terms and concepts: he entertains the possibility that we might take εὖ (well) to mean in a greatly beneficial and blessed manner. Subsequently, in I.10–21 he gives the usual meaning of "what it is to do things 'well' with regard to property management": to procure many possessions and preserve them to the best of one's ability.

10. As Jensen points out (1906, 6), Aristotle attests that the ordinary concept of οἰκονομία focuses on the acquisition of great wealth (*Eth. nic.* 1.1094a9; *Pol.* A1253b12–14). One of Philodemus's main criticisms is, precisely, that the single-minded pursuit of wealth cannot constitute a legitimate goal for the philosopher.

11. Philodemus's text is lacunose, and therefore it is difficult to sur-mise exactly how he has used Xenophon. We can tell that frag. I.1–8 corresponds to Xenophon, *Oec.* 1.4, which first talks briefly about the art (τέχνη) and ultimate goal of the property manager and then attempts to clarify the meaning of οἶκος (the household) and of possessions (κτήματα). In this context Socrates makes the paradoxical suggestion that, if every-thing one acquires belongs to the household as a possession, then also the enemies that one acquires are possessions, and the property manager makes them increase qua possessions and gets handsomely paid for it! In response, Philodemus denounces Socrates' perverse use of language as well as his sophistical spirit. Fragment I.16–19 paraphrases *Oec.* 1.5. It is worth noting that the reference to the principal meaning of κεκτῆσθαι (cf. κυ[ρίως] ὑπακουομένου τοῦ [κε]κτῆσθαι, frag. I.17–19) is Philodemus's own comment. He wants to point to the principal or "proleptic" (that is, in accord with the basic concept) meaning of "to have acquired" in order to justify his subsequent rejection of Socrates' inference in *Oec.* 1.6 that one's enemies are also things that one has acquired (cf. frag. I.19–21).

12. Fragment II is also lacunose, but, in broad lines, it seems to repro-duce *Oec.* 1.8. Only the left part of the fragment is preserved.

13. Column IIIa is a *sovrapposto*, that is, a portion of papyrus from slightly later in the scroll that has become stuck on top of the present layer. Jensen, wisely, did not attempt to supplement the text of the top lines of the column, for, as he remarks (1906, 9), very few fragments were legible in his day. Moreover, he compares IIIa.20–21 with Xenophon, *Oec.* 1.14–15. Again, in my view, we cannot be sure about this parallel, since the relevant lines in the papyrus are lacunose. At most, we may say that Philodemus cites or paraphrases some passage of Xenophon's *Oeconomicus* dealing with the good property manager and the benefits that he secures.

14. Philodemus considers futile Socrates' attempt in Xenophon's *Oeco-nomicus* to infer syllogistically (συλλο[γ]ίζεσθαι, IV.3–4) what οἰκονομία is on the basis of premises that involve departure from ordinary linguistic usage. As indicated in the introduction (xviii), Philodemus explicitly con-nects, on the one hand, Socrates' peculiar use of language with opinion (which can be true or false) and, on the other hand, ordinary linguistic usage with πρόληψις "preconception" (which can only be true). He argues that Socrates forces ordinary linguistic usage by calling "slaves" the masters of an estate and "masters" the vices that afflict them (IV.4–16); the same holds for calling rich a person whose entire estate is worth a very small sum, five minae, but poor a person whose estate is worth a hundred times more (IV.29–34; cf. also Xenophon, *Oec.* 2.1–4); since Socrates distorts the ordinary use of words to such an extent, we should infer that he cannot reach correct conclusions.

15. IV.4–8 closely paraphrases Xenophon, *Oec.* 1.19–20. There are some differences, however, that indicate either that Philodemus is using a different text from ours or that he chooses to change Xenophon's text slightly. For instance, he replaces the plural κυβεῖαι (1.20) "gambling" with the singular κυβε[ία]ν (IV.7–8) and the phrase ἀνωφελεῖς ἀνθρώπων ὁμιλίαι (1.20), "unprofitable conversations of people," with his own term κακομειλί[α]ν (IV.8; cf. *De conv.* I.2), a word referring to the kind of speech that occurs in bad society and cultivates vice. Also, in IV.8–16, corresponding to *Oec.*1.21–23, he prefers the genitive singulars λ[ιχνε]-ίας (IV.13), "gluttony," οἰνο[φλυγ]ίας (IV.13–14), "drunkenness," and φιλοτ[ι]μίας (IV.14), "ambition" to Xenophon's genitive plurals λιχνειῶν, οἰνοφλυγιῶν, and φιλοτιμιῶν (1.22), and he also drops the term λαγνειῶν (1.22), "acts of lechery," which is in Xenophon's list. It is possible that Philodemus opts for the genitive singular form because he considers it more abstract. As for the removal of lust from the list of these vices, perhaps Philodemus does not find it nearly as dangerous as the excessive love of food and drink or the love of honor. IV.25–34 reflects *Oec.* 2.1–8. In particular, IV.23–27 is probably a loose paraphrase of Critoboulos's comment that, upon reflection, he finds that he does have self-control regarding the vices that are likely to hinder the increase of his estate, so he asks Socrates to advise him as to how to increase his estate, unless Socrates believes that they are both sufficiently wealthy and not in need of money (cf. 2.1). IV.27–34 refers to Socrates' answer, which contains the paradoxical claim that Socrates himself is rich because his property of about five minae suffices for his needs, whereas Critoboulos is poor because his property of more than five hundred minae cannot sustain his lifestyle (cf. *Oec.* 2.2–4). Although Philodemus's text is damaged, there is good indication that he remains quite faithful to Xenophon's phrasing.

16. Xenophon's text contains no reference to "the necessary and natural needs of men" (cf. *De oec.* IV.7–9). The phrase is both an implicit allusion to the Epicurean division of desires (Epicurus, *Ep. Men.* 127; *Sent.*

29, 30; cf. also *De elect.* VI.1–5) and a plausible interpretation by Philodemus of the following passage.

> C. Despite your estimate (sc. Socrates' estimate that his property might be worth five minae, whereas Critoboulos's property is worth more than a hundred times that sum), you really think that you do not need any more money and pity me for my poverty?
>
> S. Yes, because my property is enough to provide what is sufficient for my needs, whereas I do not think that you would have enough to sustain your lifestyle and your reputation even if your property were three times more what it is now.
>
> C. How can this be?
>
> S. First, I observe that you are compelled to offer many large sacrifices, otherwise I think that you would have against you both gods and men. Then, it befits your position to receive many house guests and to do it with magnificence, too. Next, you have to give dinners and bestow benefits to citizens, or else you lose your allies. Furthermore, I feel that the state also makes already heavy demands upon you: to keep horses, pay for choruses, sponsor gymnastic competitions, and undertake presidencies, and if there is war, I know that they will demand of you to maintain a ship and to contribute so much money that it will nearly bankrupt you. Whenever you seem to do less lavishly one of these things, I know that the Athenians will punish you no less than if they had caught you stealing their own possessions. Besides all this, I see that you think of yourself as a rich man, and, while you are negligent as to how to make money, you devote your attention to courting youths as if the cost were nothing to you. For these reasons I pity you and fear that you may suffer irretrievable loss and be reduced to utter poverty. As for me, you know as well as I do that, if I need something more than what I have, there is no shortage of friends who will amply satisfy my needs by making some very small contribution. On the other hand, your friends aspire to receive benefits from you, although they are far better equipped than you are to support their own establishment. (Xenophon, *Oec.* 2.4–8)

In V.6–11 Philodemus reformulates the position of Xenophon's Socrates in distinctly Epicurean terms. Xenophon's Socrates says that his own property

NOTES 85

suffices to satisfy his needs: τὰ μὲν γὰρ ἐμά, ἔφη, ἱκανά ἐστιν ἐμοὶ παρέχειν τὰ ἐμοὶ ἀρκοῦντα (*Oec.* 2.4). Philodemus describes the needs in question as τἀναγκαῖα [κ]αὶ τὰ φυσικὰ τῶν ἀνθρώπων ἐπιζητήματα (V.7–9), "the necessary and natural needs of men," and he also attributes to Socrates the claim that κεν[ὴν εἶν]αι τὴν ἐν τῷ ζῆν εὐετηρίαν (V.10–11), "prosperity in life is something empty," using the Epicurean notion of empty desires and their objects. He probably derives this last claim from his interpretation of *Oec.* 2.5–8, where Socrates explains just why he calls himself rich but Critoboulos poor: Critoboulos's lifestyle consists of activities and obligations that, as Socrates implies, are both cumbersome and redundant, such as large sacrifices, public benefactions, and lavish entertainments. In Epicurean language, the desires corresponding to such objects are empty desires, and the prosperity consisting of the accomplishment of such activities is also empty—a vain, unnatural, and harmful thing.

17. On the connection between οἰκονομία and excellence (V.14–19), consider the following passages from Xenophon's *Oeconomicus*:

> I tell you this, Critoboulos, said Socrates, because even the wealthiest people cannot abstain from agriculture. For the pursuit of it seems to be a source of pleasure as well as a means of increasing one's estate and of training the body in everything that befits a free person. (4.25)

> "Pray, where do you spend your time," said I, "and what do you do when you are not engaged in some such activity? For I want very much to learn from you how you reached the point of being called a gentleman (καλός τε κἀγαθός), since you do not spend your time indoors and your physical condition does not indicate that you do so." (7.2)

Ischomachus answers that, indeed, he does not spend his time indoors but outdoors, and he gives an account of how he trained his wife to look after the house by herself (7.4–43). Toward the end of this account, he draws an explicit connection between οἰκονομία and the virtues: "Good and beautiful things, I said, are increased in human life not through outward comeliness, but through the daily exercise of the virtues" (7.43).

It is important, however, to note that [καλοκαγαθία]ν, "moral excellence" (Philodemus, *De oec.* V.19), is a conjecture.

18. Philodemus's text is lacunose, but, so far as we can tell, Philodemus remains close to Xenophon's text as we have it. VI.5 exactly reports Socrates' claim about Ischomachus, namely, that he is a gentleman, καλός τε κἀγαθὸς ἀνήρ (*Oec.* 6.12; 12.2).

19. In VI.16–18 Philodemus levels another charge against Socrates' use of language: not that he deviates from ordinary usage, losing connection with the πρόληψις (preconception) underlying each term (see nn. 14–16 above), but that he falls prey to ambiguity. This compromises his search into the nature of property management, for, according to Epicurus and his followers, the unambiguous use of terms is a prerequisite of scientific and philosophical enquiry. Philodemus's teacher, Zeno of Sidon, and his associates were especially attentive to issues concerning the multiple meanings of words.

20. On Socrates' disavowal of expertise in property management but his intention to discuss that subject nonetheless, see Xenophon, *Oec.* 2.11. VI.21–35 probably paraphrases in summary form *Oec.* 2.16–18.

21. The contents of Jensen's col. IIIb are a virtual quotation of Xenophon, *Oec.* 3.4–5 Since they are mainly invented, they were not included in the translation. The same holds for Jensen's "columna perdita," a paraphrase of Xenophon's *Oec.* 3.5. Xenophon's central idea in these passages is that good property management ensures the goodwill and productivity of slaves and the prosperity of farmers, whereas bad property management has the opposite results. Xenophon's tack on slaves is purely utilitarian: we must manage them well so that they are eager to work and unwilling to run away. For the record, it seems worth giving Jensen's text and its translation.

COLUMN IIIB PARS INFERIOR

[ἔνθα μὲν
πάντας ὡ[ς εἰπεῖν δεδεμέ-
νους, καὶ [τούτους θαμινὰ ἀπο-
διδράσκο[ν]τ[ας, ἔνθα δὲ λελυ-
μένους [καὶ ἐθέλοντάς τ' ἐρ-
γάζεσθ[αι καὶ παραμένειν,
ὥστε κα[ὶ τοῦτ' ἀξιοθέατον

οἰκονο[μίας ἔργον, καὶ παρα-
πλησίου[ς γεωργίας γεωργοῦν-
τας [τοὺς μὲν ἀπολωλέναι
φάσ[κ]ον[τας ὑπὸ τῆς γεωργίας κὰ[ποροῦντας, τοὺς δὲ ἀ-
φθόν[ως καὶ καλῶς πάντα ἔ-
χοντα[ς ἀπ' αὐτῆς ὅσων δέονται,
εἰ οἱ μὲ[ν αὐτῶν οὐκ εἰς ἃ δεῖ
μόν[ον ἀναλίσκουσιν, ἀλλὰ

Column perdita

[καὶ εἰς ἃ βλάβην φέρει αὐτοῖς καὶ τοῖς οἴκοις, οἱ δ' οὐ-
δ' εἰς τἀναγκαῖα δαπανᾶν ἔ-
χουσιν ....

Column IIIb Pars inferior

[... here all the servants are, as it were, in bonds and often running away, whereas there they are free from bonds and willing
to work and to remain in the estate; so this too is a noteworthy
achievement of property management. And as to the farmers who
cultivate similar fields, some of them declare that they are ruined
by agriculture and indeed they are reduced to poverty, whereas
others get from agriculture everything that they need in abundance and in an honorable way, if the former group of them do
not spend money only for necessary purposes but]

Column perdita

[also for aims that bring damage to themselves and to their
homes, whereas the latter group cannot afford to spend money
even for things that are necessary]

22. Column II roughly corresponds to *Oec.* 3.10–15. More specifically, II.3–8 refers to *Oec.* 3.10; II.12–16 to *Oec.* 3.11; and II.21–33 to *Oec.*
3.15. It is less clear what II.8–12 refers to. One possibility is that it corresponds to *Oec.* 3.12: Philodemus interprets Socrates asking Critoboulos

whether he holds conversations with his wife as addressing the problem whether a wife is necessary and useful for the philosophical running of the household and for the philosopher's happiness. What features of Xenophon's text may justify reading *Oec.* 3.12 in this way? Socrates and Critoboulos agree that typically the master of the estate commits more affairs of importance to his wife than to anyone else (3.12). If she is a good partner, she contributes just as much to the good of the household as her husband does (3.15). She is likely to become a good partner if she is well instructed by her husband (3.11). As Socrates suggests and Ischomachus later illustrates, that instruction occurs through conversation of the husband with his wife (cf. 3.12). So, conversation can be considered the means by which the wife becomes necessary and useful to the increase of the estate (cf. 3.15). Taken together, a husband and a well-trained wife are sufficient for that purpose (3.15). However, Philodemus's interpretation goes beyond Xenophon's text by focusing on the *philosophical* management of the household and the *philosopher's* well-being. This feature can be explained not by reference to Xenophon but to Philodemus's own agenda.

23. The content of this column roughly corresponds to *Oec.* 12.3–10.

24. XII.1–2 rejects Ischomachus's claim that he trains his bailiff himself because the bailiff does not need to know anything more than what he himself knows (*Oec.* 12.3–4). Although Philodemus alludes to some features of the bailiff's training, there is much that he omits: for instance, how Ischomachus teaches his bailiffs and how he instills in them loyalty toward himself (12.5–7); how he teaches them to be careful (12–8–10); what sorts of men are susceptible to such teaching (12.11–16); and by what method he makes them diligent (12.17–20). Either Philodemus did not have access to this material, or, more probably, he suppresses it because he considers it redundant. VII.5–8 supports this last possibility: Ischomachus's account of how he teaches the bailiffs to rule the slaves by citing examples of trained animals is, according to Philodemus, both trivial and long-winded.

25. Philodemus makes further references to Xenophon's text in order to criticize particular proposals: training the slaves not to steal their master's property (VII.14–17; cf. *Oec.* 14.1–2); teaching them how to be just (VII.21–26; cf. *Oec.* 14.3–7) with the aid of principles drawn from the laws of Dracon and of Solon and applying these principles consistently and strictly with appropriate rewards and punishments (VII.18–21; cf. *Oec.* 14.4–10); and also stressing the importance of agriculture (which Ischomachus discusses in considerable detail) for the good life (VII.29–37; cf. *Oec.* 15.3–12).

26. Philodemus dismisses some of Theophrastus's claims as impracticable, others as exaggerated or absurd, and others as irrelevant to philosophy and the philosophical life (see introduction, xv–xxiv). Nonetheless, his summary of or allusions to Xenophon are often biased by his own polemical agenda. An example is this: when Ischomachus first claims that he undertakes to teach his bailiff justice, he also explains what kind of justice it is (cf. ταύτην τὴν δικαιοσύνην, 13.3; δικαιοσύνης τῆς τοιαύτης, 14.4): as opposed to theoretical justice, it consists in obeying directives in order to be rewarded or to avoid punishment (14.3–10). So, it is a narrow, practically oriented conception of justice, which makes fairly plausible Ischomachus's claim that he can teach it to his bailiff and slaves. However, although Philodemus appears aware of the kind of justice that Ischomachus has in mind (VII.14–17), he plays it down when he contends that it is impossible to teach the bailiff the capacity of making people just (VII.21–26). In this way Philodemus's objection to Ischomachus gains force: while the idea that one can teach slaves not to steal may seem practicable, the expectation that the supervisor can be taught how to instill justice in the servants is absurd.

27. Philodemus is referring to his arguments against Xenophon: they suffice to demolish Theophrastus's views and everyone else's too. Regarding the summary and criticism of Theophrastus, Philodemus adopts strategies similar to the ones he used in connection with Xenophon. When we compare the two texts, we find that, broadly speaking, VIII.7–9 refers to 1343a5–7; VIII.9–12 to 1343a7–9; VIII.12–18 to 1343a10–18; VIII.18–40 to 1343a18–25; and VIII.40–45 to 1343a25–b1. Philodemus closely follows Theophrastus in focusing in particular on the importance that Hesiod ascribes to the role of the woman, who should or at least could be a wife—a target of Philodemus's criticism in subsequent columns. He also highlights Theophrastus's claims that agriculture is the best and most natural occupation (VIII.40–42) and that second come mining and other such occupations (VIII.42–45); these claims too are targets of subsequent criticism by Philodemus.

28. The introductory material in question constitutes the first chapter of the *Oeconomica* (1343a1–18; see also next note). It consists of a few remarks concerning the relation between the art of property management and the art of politics, and also the relation between the οἶκος (household) and the πόλις (city-state). Philodemus paraphrases and assesses these remarks in the lines that follow.

29. Philodemus concedes that Theophrastus does well to distinguish between different parts of the οἶκος (household) and to examine each of them thoroughly, for in his view these topics do belong to the discipline of οἰκονομία (property management), contrary to other topics discussed by Theophrastus that do not. Philodemus's move here is consistent with his general methodology, as he outlines it toward the end of *De oeconomia* (XXVII.12–20): if some of his rivals' tenets are useful, he must acknowledge it and include them in his own treatise.

30. Cf. Hesiod, *Op.* 406: κτητήν, οὐ γαμετήν, ἥτις καὶ βουσὶν ἔποιτο ("acquired, not married, who can follow with the oxen"). According to M. L. West (1988, ad loc.), the purpose of the line is to change the original sense of *Op.* 405: οἶκον μὲν πρώτιστα γυναῖκά τε βοῦν τ'ἀροτῆρα ("a house first of all, a woman, and an ox for plowing"). Philodemus's passage (VIII.35–40), in particular his remark that "many people say," is listed as part of the evidence that the line was not in all ancient copies of Hesiod's text. However, Philodemus's phrase "many people say" should be cited as testimony, not to the absence of the line from some copies of *Opera et dies*, but to the existence of a variant reading of the line. That is, in the copy that Philodemus is using, the line was probably there, but with the second word ἤ rather than οὐ, so that Hesiod was saying that the woman *should* or at least *could* be a wife (κτητὴν ἤ γαμετήν, "acquired or married"). I owe this last suggestion to David Sedley.

From a philosophical point of view, Philodemus is raising the following objection. Although he concedes at first that Theophrastus's analytic examination of the two parts of the household does belong to the subject of property management (see previous note), he subsequently objects to Theophrastus's interpretation of Hesiod's division of the household into two parts, humans and possessions, mainly because of the inconsistencies related to the theses that the wife is necessary to the free man and that she is an equal partner in the household. Thus it seems that, according to Philodemus, Hesiod's phrase cannot be used to support the distinction of the primary parts of the οἶκος (household) into humans and possessions or Theophrastus's justification of it. It is not clear just why Philodemus thinks so, that is, just what his argument is. It may run along the following lines. Theophrastus maintains that a wife is necessary to the free man in a sense analogous to that in which the possession of an estate is necessary to nourishment. This entails that the wife is a possession of some sort, but Hesiod's distinction of the household into a house and a woman implies the opposite, namely, that the wife is, or could be, something different from a mere possession. Moreover, Theophrastus seems to contradict himself. For, on the one hand, he says that a wife is something that a free man needs and gets, that is, a possession, but, on the other hand, he classifies the wife as a human being, not a possession. Additional problems have to do with Theophrastus's claim that the wife is of equal importance to the man regarding the administration of the household. For if she is a possession, she cannot be her husband's equal, and if she is his equal, she cannot be a possession. Hence, in order to be consistent, Theophrastus would have to drop either his belief in the equality of the spouses or the distinction between the two parts of the household, humans and possessions. In the sequel (VIII.34-5), Philodemus calls arbitrary the contention that the woman is the principal element of free men, then argues that that contention is simply not true (VIII.46-IX.3).

31. Philodemus omits Theophrastus's justification of the claim that agriculture is the most just of all occupations because the wealth it brings is acquired through one's own efforts, not through other men with or without their own consent (1343a28-31). This view of Theophrastus's lends itself to an interpretation that emphasizes its apparently altruistic concerns. If so, Philodemus has good reason to remove it, for, in his own classification of different sources of income, he advances the opposite idea, that it is preferable to earn an income through the labor of others than through one's own (see XXIII.3-21 and introduction, xxxix-xl).

32. VIII.45-IX.3 questions Theophrastus's claim that a man's wife is "of the first importance to him" on the grounds that it is possible to live a happy life without her. Theophrastus's text contains an obvious answer, namely, that, in addition to the fact that a wife is indispensable to the good running of the household, there is a natural bond between husband and wife, man and woman (1343b7-1344a7). In Epicurean terms, therefore, Theophrastus can be interpreted as saying that the wife fulfills natural or even necessary desires and needs. Since Philodemus wants to argue that, in fact, a wife is not necessary to the philosopher's happiness, he has a powerful motive to omit Theophrastus's emphasis on the naturalness of the union between spouses. Other correspondences between the two texts include the following: IX.8–9 summarizes 1344a15–17; IX.13 corresponds to 1344a23–28; IX.19–20 contains an exegetical addition to Theophrastus's text: ἀμφοτέρων καὶ ἐλευθέρων εἶναι δυναμένων, "who (sc. the bailiff and the worker) can also both be freemen"; the phrase either existed in Philodemus's copy of Theophrastus or is introduced by Philodemus for purposes of clarity; and IX.26–44 paraphrases 1344a29–34 with small changes; notably, while Theophrastus recommends that a share of honor be given to slaves who do more of the work of a freeman (τοῖς ἐλευθεριωτέροις, 1344a30), Philodemus makes the same recommendation with regard to the truer or better slaves (τοῖς [ἀ]ληθιν[ω]τέροις, IX.28–29). Again, either Philodemus is using a different text of the *Oeconomica*, or he is emending Theophrastus's text according to his own interpretation of what Theophrastus is saying.

33. Philodemus reads οἰκονομι|κώτατον (IX.12–13), the most managerial or most profitable for property management, where the manuscripts of Theophrastus's treatise have ἡγεμονικώτατον, the most profitable for leadership (1344a24). Given that Theophrastus is talking about slaves at this point, οἰκονομικώτατον seems the better reading: slaves may be good at helping in the management of the household, but, as an Aristotelian, Theophrastus would not want to say that they are useful for leadership. Most editors of Theophrastus's text (e.g., Armstrong 1935; van Groningen and Wartelle 1968) follow Philodemus's reading.

34. Columns X, XI, and the beginning of XII also contain loose paraphrases of Theophrastus as well as Philodemus's criticisms: IX.44–X.28 refers to 1344a35–1345b22; X.28–34 to 1344b22–27; XI.3–41 to 1344b27–1345a17; and XI.41–XII.2 to 1345a33–b1. It is worth noting that Philodemus does not mention the contents of 1343a18–35. This omission seems again motivated by his own philosophical standpoint, for Theophrastus's passage talks about how to dispose of the produce of large estates; how to use and how to inspect goods and implements; how to provide and care for the stock, the crops, and the accommodation of the slaves; and how to choose the right type of house, its shape, orientation, and so forth. Philodemus makes it clear that he considers such details trivial as

well as irrelevant to his own project. One may wonder why the principles that one must not take into one's household races that are too cowardly or too high-spirited and that one must reward hard-working slaves with prizes are more relevant to philosophical οἰκονομία (cf. μᾶλλον δέ in X.7–8) than the precepts concerning the disproportionate punishment of slaves (X.2–7). Philodemus explains that, although the latter do pertain to the philosopher, they should not be used in connection with the treatment of one's slaves, for otherwise several other similar points ought to be raised as well in that connection. But this holds true of the former pair of principles as well. Besides, they appear vulnerable to the objection that they do not concern the philosopher more than the common man (cf. IX.44–X.2).

35. Philodemus questions the legitimacy of including arrangement (τὸ κοσμητικόν) in the kinds of activities constituting traditional property management (acquisition, preservation, arrangement, and use). However, he himself appears ambivalent about it. On the one hand, he objects that arranging the possessions as one should and where one should is reducible to their acquisition and preservation; it is not a distinct kind of activity. On the other hand, he concedes for the sake of the argument that arrangement adds pleasure to utility in ways in which the other three "most necessary" activities do not; on that count arrangement also belongs to the domain of property management.

36. Philodemus has good hedonic grounds for rejecting the Persian method of supervising personally the management of one's household and estate. However, it is less obvious why he objects to the Attic method of "purchasing at the same time as one sells" and calls that method "troublesome" and "unprofitable." One possibility is that he objects to exchanges as such, in particular exchanges that involve the use of money. Another possibility is that, in Philodemus's view, the pressure to buy and sell while keeping nothing in store (cf. Theophrastus, *Oec.* 1344b33–34) causes anxiety and may force us to make bad deals.

37. XII.3 signals the end of this part of Philodemus's treatise. The papyrus contains a *coronis* indicating the transition from the first, dialectical part of the work to the second, chiefly expository part.

38. The concept of the measure of wealth (πλούτου μέ[τρ]ον, XII.18–19) is related to that of natural wealth (φυσικὸς πλοῦτος), and both are traced back to Epicurus and his associates (cf. Philodemus's reference to the leaders, καθηγεμόνες, in XII.20–22). Natural wealth has a proper measure in virtue of the fact that it satisfies the kinds of desire that also have a proper measure: a natural and necessary or merely natural desire (Epicurus, *Kyriai Doxai* 15; *Ep. Men.* 130). Philodemus implies that there were several treatises *On Wealth* in circulation, composed by authorities of the school (XII.21–22). One of them is Metrodorus's treatise (see Diogenes Laertius, *Vitae* 10.24), to which Philodemus subsequently refers in some detail. Philodemus's own work *On Wealth* (*De divitiis*, PHerc. 163, edited by Tepedino-Guerra 1978) probably developed and interpreted some earlier themes, but only a few fragments of it survive.

39. The debate between Metrodorus and the Cynics focuses on the issue whether wealth has any value and, if it does, of what kind. While the Cynics are staunch advocates of πενία or πτωχεία, "poverty or penury," denying that wealth has any value at all, Metrodorus treats it as an instrumental good whose practical value is determined by its good or bad use. His position is closer to Zeno's position than one might expect: like Zeno and other Stoics, Metrodorus views (natural) wealth as a preferred indifferent of some sort. Philodemus highlights that aspect when he suggests that, on the one hand, the wise man will be hopeful and content with a frugal life, but, on the other hand, "he feels more inclined, prompted by his will, toward a more affluent way of living" (XVI.4–6). Woolf (2009) argues that this was Epicurus's position as well.

40. The first-person plural (ὡς προείπαμεν, XIII.33–34) indicates that Philodemus speaks in his own voice, paraphrasing and developing Metrodorus's doctrine. He does so in a number of places, in which he also signals his departure from the letter of Metrodorus's account. Hence, in my view, columns XII–XXII are not a verbatim copy of Metrodorus but chiefly contain Philodemus's own take on that earlier material (see Tsouna-McKirahan 1996). In general, he approaches the matter of οἰκονομία (property management) in a more systematic and technical manner than Metrodorus, which is partly shaped by the socioeconomic context of the late Republic and by the ongoing philosophical debates on property management among the late Hellenistic schools.

41. Philodemus's own voice is entirely explicit, as the first-person singular indicates (see νομίζω, XIV.29–30). In the passage that follows he focuses primarily on the sage's emotional detachment from gains and losses, the correct calculation and balance of pains and pleasures, and the importance of friendship in decisions related to the preservation of wealth.

42. Delattre's conjecture is compatible with the traces on the papyrus, though there remains some uncertainty as to the width of the lacuna toward the beginning of XIV.32. On Jensen's reconstruction of the text (πρὸ[s βί]αν ἕλκειν ἑαυ[τόν], XIV.32), the translation would be "dragging oneself by force" or, more loosely, "pushing oneself too hard."

43. XIV.46–XV.3 suggests that there is an indissoluble link between the property management "of the wise man and his capacity for friendship." Assuming that ἑτοιμότης refers to, among other things, dispositional traits, his desire for κτῆσις (the acquisition of goods) is virtually one and the same (cf. ἀπαρά[λλα]|κτος: XIV.46–XV.1) as his desire to share his goods with others.

44. The emendation <δεδιόσι> (XV.13) is explicable by haplography: the following word (δεομέ|[νω]ν, XV.13–14) also begins with δε-.

45. It is unclear whom Philodemus has in mind here. The next phrase (XV.14–21) states that, if the individuals in question engage exclusively with those who have a noisy way of earning their living, they find themselves in want of things conducive to their goal. So, perhaps Philodemus is referring to sophists and their victims. On the present reconstruction of the text, the meaning seems to be this: people who are at the mercy of sophists and are intimidated by their fallacious arguments may be led to spend too much money at times when there is none; generally they make bad choices and acquire fewer things conducive to wealth or pleasure.

46. The desire for "a more affluent way of living" is probably a natural but not necessary desire. See also XVI.30–32 and notes 38 and 39.

47. Note that this argument cannot be intended to attack the Cynics. Its point is not that natural wealth is preferable to poverty but rather that the sage can live well *even if* he happens to lose his wealth. On my interpretation, this argument as well as the surrounding context should not be attributed to Metrodorus but to Philodemus. See Tsouna-McKirahan 1996 and note 40 above.

48. See note 46.

49. I follow Jensen's reconstruction of these lines for lack of a better solution, but the text is almost certainly corrupt. The μή (XII.2) should be οὐ, the participle προειρημένοις should be preceded by τοῖς, and, as an instrumental dative, it is an unlikely way of expressing reasons for a contention. Philosophically, Metrodorus's views that we should seek natural wealth and that there is a proper measure of wealth indicate that he may have to some extent addressed the problem of what the philosopher ought to do with great wealth. The issue becomes much more pressing for Philodemus, in part because of philosophical criticism, in part because of the socioeconomic conditions of his Roman audience. Piso and his friends, for instance, might wonder whether the philosophical life is compatible with the possession of estates as vast as their own.

50. As mentioned also in the introduction (xxix–xxx), it is plausible to think that the love of money (φιλοχρηματία; cf. φιλοχρημάτου, XVII.13) is the vice standing opposite to the virtue exhibited by the good property manager. But what might that virtue be? One answer could be that it is not a single virtue but a cluster of virtues, all of them instantiated in the philosophical manager. Another response is that the virtue corresponding to the vice of φιλοχρηματία (the love of money) is, precisely, the disposition to administer one's property well, namely, to administer it according to the principles of the Epicurean philosophical life.

51. The Epicureans standardly opt for lower as opposed to higher forms of the same art (τέχνη). As Philodemus indicates (XVII.14–16), this happens in the case of many arts, including property management as well as, for instance, grammar and music. It is relevant, I think, to mention in this connection the Epicurean attitude toward different methods of argumentation: they prefer ἐπιλογισμός, a kind of inductively based common or garden type of reasoning, to indirect inference or analogical reasoning, and they maintain that the former is prior to and more fundamental than the latter.

52. In XVIII.7–31 Philodemus addresses the following worries. Will not the fact that the Epicurean οἰκονόμος (property manager) is not mainly concerned with the acquisition but rather with the preservation and management of his property cause him to be poor? Besides, does not the

preservation of property require assiduous work just as much as its acquisition does? Philodemus answers both questions in the negative, thus
supporting his contention that the wise man cannot reasonably be called a
bad manager even if he is not an expert.

53. The obsessive use of numbers to calculate quantities of possessions is considered a mark of greed; see also Xenophon, *Symp.* 4.45. In
the context of Philodemus's discussion, it can also be taken as a criterion
for expertise. Contrast the philosophical property manager, who is an
expert in measuring the useful and in weighing pleasures against pains
(XVIII.40–XIX.4).

54. The phrase appears to allude to both the concept of natural wealth and the third principle of the so-called Fourfold Medicine
(τετραφάρμαχος: Philodemus, [*Ad contub.*] V.9–10; see also *De elect.* XI.6–
7), according to which the good is easy to get. A few external goods suffice
to fulfill our natural desires, and these goods are readily available.

55. Philodemus may be telling us something important about the
limits of his humanitarian and philanthropic commitments: in the end,
concern for one's own pleasure carries, in his view, greater weight than
concern for others. Although the philosopher will make sure that he does
not engage in property management as an expert, he will not mind ben-
efiting occasionally from the work of such experts. Philodemus's remarks
concerning certain sources of income, such as mining and agriculture,
point in the same direction. Note that in all these cases he appears to
assume that the person who wishes to live the philosophical life owns a
substantial estate, complete with slaves, and also is probably using the ser-
vices of a professional property manager as well.

56. It is unclear who the sophists in question are. One possibility is
that Philodemus does not have any particular group of people in mind
but that he uses "sophist" and its cognates generically as derogatory terms.
In this passage he calls sophists those who use ordinary language in an
improper manner to defend a false thesis (XX.1–8). In a later passage
(XIII.32–36) he contrasts the sage's discourses with the speeches of sophists and demagogues—whom I take to be mainly teachers or practitioners
of forensic and political rhetoric. See also next note.

57. According to the Epicureans, customary linguistic usage usually guides us safely in keeping words correlated with the things that they are intended to designate; it can do so because ordinary use usually encapsulates the preconception corresponding to each term. But, as Philodemus indicates, this is not always the case. Sophists exploit ordinary usage (cf. συ[ν|ηθ]ειῶν, XX.3–4) to lend to the expression "the good moneymaker" a meaning that, in fact, it should not have (cf. XX.1–8 and note 56). Further, those who pretend to be philosophers appeal, not to the preconception as they ought to, but to conventional ways of talking, in order to apply the predicate "the good moneymaker" to the wrong kind of person (XX.45–XXI.12; see also XXI.18–22). Ordinary usage may become misleading because of many factors. One of them is the equivocal nature of language, of which Philodemus and his teachers are well aware. Another is the effect of perverted social values and habits.

58. "The method indicated above" (i.e., in XX.1–32) is the settlement of ethical disputes by appealing to the relevant preconception.

59. The traces on the papyrus seem to me to support Jensen's conjecture δ[ιδ]άσκειν (XXI.22) over Delattre's δ[όξα]ν σχεῖν.

60. Gellias was a very wealthy citizen of Acragas whose spirit, according to Valerius Maximus (*Fact.* 4.8 ext. 2), exceeded even his wealth. He died sword in hand, when Acragas was destroyed by the Carthaginians in 406/405 B.C.E. Scopas from Trichonion in Thessaly repeatedly held the office of στρατηγός (general) and, in that capacity, conducted many wars. Notably, in 220/219 he planned and led the war against the Hellenic League. In 202 B.C.E. he recruited and commanded an army on behalf of King Ptolemy V of Egypt. However, after losing the battle of Paneion in 200 B.C.E., he was besieged in Sidon, then taken to court in Alexandria by Aristomenes in 198 B.C.E. After the trial he committed suicide or was poisoned (Polybius, *Hist.* 18.53–54). Cimon, son of Miltiades, was the most important Athenian army commander and politician in the 470s and 460s B.C.E. He was repeatedly elected στρατηγός and commanded the armed forces of the Delian League in virtually all the military operations between 476 and 463 B.C.E. However, he also acquired powerful domestic enemies, and, due to his failed policy toward Sparta in 462 B.C.E., he was discredited and ostracised. Eventually he returned to Athens, participated in the campaign to recapture Cyprus, and died there, ingloriously, of plague. Nicias, one of the most important Athenian commanders of the Peloponesian war and a στρατηγός who typically acted with circumspection and care, was chosen to command the Sicilian expedition together with Lamachus and Alcibiades. Nicias had initially opposed that expedition and, after Alcibiades defected and Lamachus fell in battle, he was no longer decisive enough to advance the war. After a severe defeat, he tried to escape with his army but had to surrender and was executed by the Syracusans (Thucydides, *Hist.* 7.84–86). Philodemus uses these exempla to illustrate his point that a military career is not an appropriate source of income for the philosopher, because it involves vastly more pains than pleasures; authors who praise the achievements of military men gloss over the fact that many of them are eventually discredited and/or die a painful death (see also introduction, xxxvii–xxxviii).

61. Aristotle maintains that the art of war is a natural art of acquisition and that war conducted against people who are intended by nature to be governed is naturally just (*Pol.* 1.8 1256b22–25).

62. It is uncertain which opponents Philodemus has in mind here. Probably they are authors of *Lives*, that is, biographies of eminent people, but Philodemus does not name them. If they use the distinction to which Philodemus alludes (XXII.25–26), between practical and contemplative wisdom and between the practical and contemplative lives, it is likely that they belong to the Peripatetic tradition. The claims of these opponents and Philodemus's answer to them are discussed in the introduction (xxxviii).

63. Philodemus does not explain why it is "[extremely] ridiculous" (XXIII.1) to consider the equestrian art an appropriate source of revenues. Compare Xenophon, *Oec.* 3.8:

C. You think me ridiculous, don't you, Socrates?
   S. You think yourself far more so, he said. Now suppose I show you that some people have been brought to utter poverty by keeping horses, whereas others prosper for doing so and are thrilled at their gain?
   C. Indeed, I too see and know instances of both, but that does not make me more one of the gainers.

64. Philodemus appears to think that the "madness" (μανικόν, XXIII.7) of the person who earns a living by his own efforts at mining is considerably worse than his earning a living by the efforts of his servants (cf. the milder characterization οὐκ εὔκληρον at XXIII.5). Again, it would seem that what the philosopher should not accept for himself, he may tolerate and even desire for others. See also note 55.

65. Recall Epicurus's claim that the wise man "will love the countryside" (φιλαγρήσειν: Diogenes Laertius, *Vitae* 10.120). As mentioned (note 55), Philodemus's remarks concerning agriculture as a source of income also appear to follow an egoistic line of thought.

66. See Diogenes Laertius, *Vitae* 10.121: "he (the wise man) will make money only by his wisdom, should he be in poverty."

67. See note 56.

68. Despite Philodemus's earlier criticisms of Xenophon's Socrates (IV.1–16), this passage has an oddly Socratic ring. Philodemus extends the meaning of the activities of acquisition and preservation of property to include the management of desires and fears, just as Xenophon's Socrates does (*Oec.* 1.22–23).

69. Recall that Xenophon and Theophrastus, as well as Philodemus, consider justice and lawfulness essential features of the activities of the good property manager. Here, then, Philodemus is not countering the view of his philosophical rivals but rather a belief widespread among the many.

70. In this column and the next Philodemus advances a thoroughly instrumental view of friendship. However, elsewhere in his ethical works he makes room for disinterested friendship and concern for others. For a substantiation of this view see Tsouna 2007, 27–31 and *passim*.

71. A proverbial phrase; see, for instance, Plato, *Gorg.* 499c; *Leg.* 12 959c. Usually it means "make the best of the circumstances," "take advantage of the opportunity at hand." However, to the extent that it might seem to dictate a *carpe diem* attitude, Philodemus objects to it. Rather than living only for the day, the good Epicurean should also focus his attention on the past and future. Concerning the acquisition and preservation of possessions, Philodemus recommends looking to the future and relates this attitude to the correct performance of the hedonistic calculus and to the lasting value of friendship. More generally, elsewhere he dissociates a *carpe diem* attitude from the true enjoyment of present pleasures (*De elect.* XVII.3–20) and emphasizes the moral relevance of the future (*De elect.* XIV.5, XXII.17–21, XXIII.7–13).

72. It is worth noting Philodemus's sensitivity regarding the way in which one's purchases, expenses, and so forth are perceived by others. The fact that he makes social perceptions a factor that regulates in part one's expenditures must have had particular appeal to his elite Roman audience. See also XXV.37–XXVI.1, in which he explicitly criticizes "some Romans" (XXV.38) for failing to realize that one should be flexible about expenditures, because circumstances and social requirements occasionally give rise to unanticipated needs.

73. Although there is room for an extra letter in XXV.33, nonetheless I prefer Jensen's κα[τά]||γειν to Delattre's κα[ταρ]||γεῖν (XXV.33–34) for reasons of sense.

74. These measures are suggested by Xenophon.

> Indeed, you will have to do these things, I said. You will remain indoors and send out those servants whose work is outdoors; check on those who should work indoors; receive the incomings; distribute as much of them as needs to be spent, but make provision and preserve so much as should be kept in store, so that the sum laid by for a year be not spent within the month. (*Oec.* 7.35)

> We also put by themselves the things consumed on a monthly basis, and we set apart the provisions calculated to last for a year. For in this way it is less likely to slip our attention how they will last as long as they must. (9.8)

75. Why does Philodemus recommend that retrenchments should affect oneself more than one's friends? One possible motivation may be altruism: although earlier passages point in the opposite direction, this passage suggests that one should care less for one's own needs and more for the needs of others. An alternative motivation is the pleasure that one gets from addressing the needs of one's friends first. Yet another possibility, compatible with Philodemus's expressed concern for decorum in the previous column, is that the recommended practice will meet with social approval.

76. Delattre plausibly maintains that "conversation" refers to the conversation between Socrates and Ischomachus.

77. See also XI.3–21. In both passages Philodemus criticizes specific tenets put forward by Theophrastus.

78. This passage alludes to two topics that Philodemus discusses in the treatise *On Death*: the composition of wills and the idea that a right-thinking person should treat his friends as heirs, especially if he does not have children of his own. On my interpretation (see Tsouna 2007, 283–85), Philodemus's attitude to wills is not that we should not have postmortem desires or leave instructions concerning the disposition of our property after death, but rather that we should write our wills in the right spirit, that is, fully realizing the vulnerability of our plans to the turns of fortune (see *De mort.* XXIV.31–XXV.2). As for bequeathing our property to our friends, especially in case we are childless, Philodemus argues that we should find consolation in the prospect that our inheritance may be passed on to people both beloved and good (*De mort.* XXIV.10–17). On the subject of wills, see Fitzgerald 2003; Warren 2004, 191–200; Tsouna 2007; and Henry 2010, xv–xxii.

79. This is a very important passage. On the one hand, Philodemus appeals to the authority of Metrodorus to defend the philosophical value of his own treatise and his detailed engagement with its subject. On the other hand, he openly acknowledges that the matter of οἰκονομία (property management) is more pressing for him than it was for Metrodorus. This seems to me to support my earlier suggestion (developed in Tsouna-McKirahan 1996) that most of the material in columns XII–XXII focusing on οἰκονομία (property management) proper does *not* belong to Metrodorus but is introduced by Philodemus.

80. Note the contrast between κατὰ [μέρος], "many details" (XXVIII.2), and ὁλοσχερεστέρων, "the most general principles" (XXVII.49).

Bibliography

Armstrong, G. Cyril, trans. 1935. Aristotle, *Oeconomica*. Loeb Classical Library. Cambridge: Harvard University Press.

Audring, Gert, and Kai Brodersen, eds. and trans. 2008. *Oikonomika: Quellen zur Wirtschaftstheorie der griechischen Antike.* Texte zur Forschung 92. Darmstadt: Wissenschaftliche Buchgesellschaft.

Blank, David L. 1985. Socratics versus Sophists on Payment for Teaching. *Classical Antiquity* 4:1–49.

———. 1995. Philodemus on the Technicity of Rhetoric. Pages 178–88 in *Philodemus and Poetry: Poetic Theory and Practice in Lucretius, Philodemus, and Horace*. Edited by Dirk Obbink. Oxford: Oxford University Press.

Cavallo, Guglielmo. 1983. *Libri scritture scribi a Ercolano: Introduzione allo studio dei materiali greci*. Cronache Ercolanesi 13 supp. 1. Naples: Macchiaroli.

Fitzgerald, John T. 2003. Last Wills and Testaments in Graeco-Roman Perspective. Pages 639–72 in *Early Christianity and Classical Culture: Comparative Studies in Honor of Abraham J. Malherbe*. Edited by John T. Fitzgerald. Thomas H. Olbricht, and L. Michael White. Supplements to Novum Testamentum 110. Leiden: Brill.

Gaisford, Thom. 1824. *Herculanensium Voluminum pars I*. Oxford: Clarendon.

Gigante, Marcello. 1995. *Philodemus in Italy: The Books from Herculaneum*. Translated by Dirk Obbink. Ann Arbor: University of Michigan Press.

Göttling, Karl Wilhelm. 1830. Ἀριστοτέλους Οἰκονομικός. Ἀνωνύμου Οἰκονομικά. Φιλοδήμου Περὶ κακιῶν καὶ τῶν ἀντικειμένων ἀρετῶν θ'. Jena: Walz.

Groningen, Bernhard Abraham van, and André Wartelle, eds. 1968. *Aristotle, Économique*. Paris: Belles-Lettres.

Hartung, Johann Adam. 1857. *Philodems Abhandlungen über die Haushaltung und über den Hochmut und Theophrasts Haushaltung und Charakterbilder, griechisch und deutsch, mit kritischen und erklärenden Anmerkungen*. Leipzig: Engelmann.

Henry, W. Benjamin, trans. 2010. *Philodemus, On Death*. Writings from the Greco-Roman World 29. Atlanta: Society of Biblical Literature.

Hopper, Robert John. 1979. *Trade and Industry in Classical Greece*. Aspects of Greek and Roman Life. London: Thames & Hudson.

Javarone, Francesco, ed. 1827. [PHerc. 1424]. Pages 1–55 in *Herculanensium voluminum quae supersunt tomus III*. Naples: Regia Typographia.

Jensen, Christian, ed. 1906. *Philodemi Περὶ οἰκονομίας qui dicitur libellus*. Bibliotheca scriptorum graecorum et romanorum teubneriana. Leipzig: Teubner.

Laurenti, Renato. 1973. *Filodemo e il pensiero economico degli Epicurei*. Milan: Istituto editoriale cisalpino La Goliardica.

Longo Auricchio, Francesca. 1977. Φιλοδήμου Περὶ ῥητορικῆς *libros primum et secundum*. Ricerche sui papiri ercolanesi 3. Naples: Giannini.

Natali, Carlo. 1995. Oikonomia in Hellenistic Political Thought. Pages 95–128 in *Justice and Generosity: Studies in Hellenistic Social and Political Philosophy*. Edited by André Laks and Malcolm Schofield. Cambridge: Cambridge University Press.

Perron, Heinrich. 1895. Textkritische Bemerkungen zu Philodems Oeconomicus. Ph.D. dissertation, University of Zurich.

Schömann, Georg Friedrich. 1839. *Specimen observationum in Theophrasti Oeconomicum et Philodemi librum IX de virtutibus et vitiis*. Gryphiswaldiae: Koch.

Sider, David. 1997. *The Epigrams of Philodemos*. New York: Oxford University Press.

Tepedino-Guerra, Adele. 1978. Il primo libro sulla ricchezza di Filodemo. *Cronache Ercolanesi* 8:52–95.

Tsouna, Voula. 2007. *The Ethics of Philodemus*. Oxford: Oxford University Press.

Tsouna-McKirahan, Voula. 1996. Epicurean Attitudes to Management and Finance. Pages 701–14 in vol. 2 of *Epicureismo greco e romano: Atti del congresso internazionale, Napoli, 19–26 maggio 1993*. Edited by Gabriele Giannantoni and Marcello Gigante. 3 vols. Naples: Bibliopolis.

Warren, James. 2004. *Facing Death: Epicurus and His Critics*. Oxford: Clarendon.

West, M. L., trans. 1988. *Hesiod: Theogony; and, Works and Days*. Oxford: Oxford University Press.

Woolf, Raphael. 2009. Pleasure and Desire. Pages 158–78 in *The Cambridge Companion to Epicureanism*. Edited by James Warren. Cambridge: Cambridge University Press.

Index Verborum

In compiling this index, I have included only what seems likely to have been in the original text. All verbs are given in their present active infinitive (or middle/passive for deponent verbs), and adjectives and adverbs in their positive form. Only the most irregular comparatives and superlatives have received separate entries. If a word is largely or wholly contained within square or angled brackets in the edited text, I have indicated this by placing the line numbers in which the word appears within the relevant brackets. If a word runs over a line end, the word is indexed under the line in which the word ends or is likely to have ended. Where the text quotes Theophrastus, Xenophon, and so forth, the source is indicated. I have omitted δέ, καί, μέν, τε, and the article.

δέσποινα 4.23
δεσπόσυνος 7.17
δεσπότης [B.2], 4.4, 4.12
δεύτερος 23.23
δέχεσθαι 8.36, 13.35, 16.46
δή fr. 2.9, 5.14, 7.37, 17.6, 18.7, 21.35, 27.20, 27.35
δῆλος 7.37, 13.19, 18.47, 22.43
δημιουργός 17.17
δημοκοπικός 23.35
δήποτε [6.26]
διά + acc. [8.34], 8.46, 9.8, 9.21, 10.7, 14.1, 14.25, 18.44, 19.1, 19.21
διά + gen. A.24, 6.15, 2.28, [2.30], 7.36, 15.3, 15.39, 18.5, [20.2], 23.33, 23.35
διαγωγή 12.32, 14.4, 22.16, 23.14
διάθεσις [B.13], 24.34
διαθεωρεῖν 19.6
διαιρεῖν [A.7]
δίαιτα 16.3, 23.46, 28.7
διακεῖσθαι 15.7, 16.20, 22.5
διακόσμησις 11.1
διαλαμβάνειν 21.36
διαλέγειν 7.39, 12.6
διάλεξις 26.32
διαλλάττειν 7.45
διαμενεῖν 1.13
διαμερίζειν [B.15]
διανιστάναι [B.8], 11.38
διανύειν 12.38
διαπίπτειν 17.37
διασώζειν 15.34
διατακτικός 17.43
διατάττειν 25.33
διαφέρειν 8.1, 12.13, 18.2, 18.27, 19.44
διαψεύδειν 26.37

διδάσκαλος 6.8
διδάσκειν 3a.14, 6.13, 2.14, 7.6, 7.16, 7.24, 21.22, 21.27
διέξοδος 28.3
δίκαιος 7.22, 13.46
δικαιοσύνη 24.17
διό 8.16, 8.23, 8.41, 9.36
διοικεῖν 15.4, 16.4, 27.26
διοίκησις 16.24, 21.3
διοικονομεῖν 3a.12
διόπερ 20.16
διορίζειν 13.22
διότι 7.37, 10.8, 10.26, 19.18, 22.1
Δίων [A.21]
δοκεῖν 7.15, 10.18, 24.20, [24.46], 26.14, 26.35, 27.3, 27.37
δοξάζειν 7.26, 24.6
δοξαστικός 5.3
δοξοσκόπος 22.24
δορίκτητος 22.20
δοῦλος <4.12>, 9.14, 9.17, [9.28], 9.39, 10.24 (Xenophon), 23.4, 23.20
Δράκων 7.20
δύναμις 7.40, 9.41, 17.7, 17.12, 22.47
δύνασθαι 9.2, 9.20, 13.25, 15.16, 15.43, 18.18, 19.5, 21.46, 26.46
δυνατός 2.12, 7.22, 12.33, 20.23, 27.46
δύο 9.17
δυσχέρεια 14.7, 14.39
δυσχερής 11.24, 14.17, 14.44, 18.24, 19.16, 27.3
ἐάν 15.8, 25.30
ἐᾶν 9.27
ἑαυτοῦ see αὑτοῦ
ἐγείρειν [B.2], 11.33
ἐγκεῖσθαι 14.28

114   PHILODEMUS, *ON PROPERTY MANAGEMENT*

ἐπιτήδειος   26.19, 26.30
ἐπιτηδεύειν   7.10, 19.29, 23.37
ἐπιτροπεύειν   11.30
ἐπίτροπος   7.13, 7.24, 9.18, 26.20
ἐπιφέρειν   10.45, 14.6, 22.42
ἐπιφορά   26.1
Ἐπίχαρμος   25.8
ἐργάζεσθαι   4.9, 11.17, 11.18, 23.4
ἐργασία   [A.9], 11.12
ἐργαστικός   9.44
ἐργάτης   9.9, 9.31, 17.3, 18.32, 19.28, 22.38
ἔργον   1.5, 3a.13, 5.13, [7.36], 9.24, [9.45], 10.4, 10.9, 12.1 (Theophrastus)
Ἕρμαρχος   25.1
ἑρμηνεία   6.16, 20.3
ἔρχεσθαι   2.26
ἔσχατος   26.38
ἕτερος   12.13, 13.23 (twice)
ἔτι   [A.1], 2.12, 7.27, 18.2, 19.30
ἑτοιμότης   15.2
ἔτος   25.34
εὖ   1.6, 1.8, 1.9, 1.15, [2.31], 25.7 (Epicharmus)
εὐδαίμων   9.3
εὔελπις   25.13
εὐελπιστία   26.43
εὐετηρία   5.11, 22.3
εὐήθης   [2.35]
εὐθαρρής   [16.2]
εὔθετος   26.26
εὐθυμία   9.42
εὐθύς   14.35
εὐθυσία   10.22 (Xenophon)
εὔκληρος   23.5
εὔκολος   19.19
εὔνοια   24.24
εὐπαθεῖν   18.44

εὔπορος   16.46
εὑρίσκειν   3a.16, 15.10, 16.7
εὐστάλεια   23.41
εὔσχημος   23.18, 26.17
εὔσχολος   23.16
εὐτελής   12.34
εὐτυχεῖν   24.29
εὐφραίνειν   25.14
εὐχάριστος   23.28
εὔωνος   [25.27]
ἐφαρμόζειν   21.5
ἐφεξῆς   7.29
ἐφήμερος   14.14, 15.23
ἐφιστάναι   fr. 1.9
ἐφόδιος   15.25, 16.13, [27.8]
ἐφορᾶν   11.26
ἔχειν   [3a.21], 4.4, 5.6, 5.22, 2.4, 2.16, 10.27, 11.16, 12.39, 13.7, 13.13, 13.32, 13.36, [13.40], 13.44, 15.22, 15.26, 16.13, 21.9, 22.41, 23.10, 23.12, 23.21, 27.7
ἐχθρός   [fr. 1.19]
ζῆλος   24.7
ζηλοῦν   20.41
ζημιοῦν   24.30
ζῆν   5.10, 13.25, 16.14
ζητεῖν   3a.16, 7.2, 11.39, 21.5
ζήτριον   14.28
ζωή   9.3, 14.22
ζῷον   7.7
ἤ   [4.15], 2.16, 9.25 (twice), 9.39 (twice), 10.7, 10.24 (Xenophon), 14.21, 14.36 (twice), [14.45], 15.27, 17.22, 18.28, 19.39, 22.41, 22.45, [22.46], 23.20, 26.8, 26.47
ἡγεῖσθαι   7.25, 20.43, 22.47, 23.40
ἥδεσθαι   20.30
ἤδη   [2.34], 12.43, 19.13

νέμειν [A.10], 11.13
Νικίας 22.23
νοεῖν 1.4, 9.6, 12.11
νομίζειν 2.22, 7.2, 10.28, 14.30, 24.12
νομικός 7.20
νόμισμα 25.25
νόος 5.14
νύκτωρ B.8, 11.38
νῦν 1.18, 4.17, [21.17], 25.12
νύξ B.6, 11.41
Ξενοφῶν 6.6, 7.28, 10.19, 27.14
ὅδε 25.27 [twice], [25.28], 25.31
ὅθεν 19.6
οἴεσθαι 22.18, 23.3, 24.35
οἰκεῖν 1.6, 1.8, 1.15, 1.16, 3a.14, [3a.19]
οἰκεῖος A.23, 7.35, 8.45
οἰκέτης [B.3], 10.6, 11.32, 26.28, 26.31
οἰκία [B.5], fr. 1.16, [2.27], 8.16, 8.20, [8.24], 11.36, [23.45]
οἰκονομεῖν 6.19, 14.29, [16.33], 16.44
οἰκονομία A.14, [A.18], [B.1], B.10, 1.5, fr. 1.13, 5.18, 2.11, 9.7, 9.11, 11.28, 12.10, 15.12, 16.37, 20.37, 21.39, 21.45, 26.23, 27.11, 27.22, 27.43
οἰκονομικός 6.5, [6.13], 7.29, 7.47, 8.5, 8.17, 8.19, 9.13, 11.2, 12.11, 12.23
οἰκονόμος 3a.7, 3a.27, 10.30, 16.22, 21.41
οἶκος 1.6, 1.16, fr. 1.8, 3a.14, 3a.19, [4.12], 2.24, 2.33, 8.27 (Theophrastus, citing Hesiod), [8.33], 12.6, 16.32
οἶνος 9.33

οἰνοφλυγία 4.14
οἷος [3a.16], 6.3, 13.20, 16.20, 17.21, 18.31, 22.21, 27.9
οἱοσδήποτε 13.33
ὀλιγάκις 9.39
ὀλίγος 14.22, 18.5, 18.38, 19.19, 25.22, 25.25, 27.37
ὀλίος see ὀλίγος
ὅλος [B.4], 11.35, 13.38, 21.2, 22.28
ὁλοσχερής 27.49
ὁμαλός 26.37
ὁμιλία 21.11
ὁμοεθνής 10.15
ὅμοιος A.22, [B.18], 7.26, 8.44, 10.3
ὁμοιότροπος 24.2
ὄνομα 12.14
ὁποῖος 18.46
ὅπως [A.10], 11.13, 20.39
ὁρᾶν 15.26, 16.40, 17.21, 20.38
ὄρεξις 26.4
ὀρθός 2.18, 14.29
ὁρίζειν 10.13, 27.47
ὅς 1.18, fr. 1.21, [3a.12], 4.2, 4.14, 6.3, 6.11, 6.26, 2.21, 7.5, 7.31, 7.43, 7.45, [7.46], 8.8, 9.15, 9.22, 10.27, 11.2, 11.21, [12.9], 12.19, 12.34, 12.46, 13.5, 13.27, 13.30, 13.35, 14.16, 14.22, 14.42, 15.20, 16.8, 17.8, 17.11, 17.16, 17.39, 18.28, 18.36, [20.13], 20.47, 21.8, 23.12, 23.36, 24.25, 25.18, 25.26, 25.28, 26.45, 27.33
ὅσος [A.24], fr. 1.7, [fr. 1.17], 14.10, 16.26, 19.37, 22.39, 24.8, 26.16
ὅσπερ 12.39, 18.44, 21.28
ὅστις 7.3

[20.1], 20.21, 20.38, [21.30], 26.41, 27.44, 28.6

πόθεν 22.7

ποιεῖν [A.25], 1.7, 1.16, fr. 1.8, 3a.19, [4.12], 7.12, 7.23, 8.9, 9.36, 10.23 (Xenophon), 11.20, 13.24, 14.41, 15.38, 17.25, 18.39 (twice), 19.23, 19.39, 20.8, 21.4, 21.16, 22.5, 22.21, 24.13, 24.22, 24.31, 25.7 (Epicharmus), 25.13, 25.15, 25.39, 26.38, 27.28, 28.1

ποικίλος 26.35

ποιός 21.2, 21.39

πολέμιος [4.16], 4.24

πόλις [B.6], 8.16, 22.47

πολιτικός [8.1], 8.3, 8.18, 22.30

πολλάκις [11.29], 22.32, 24.32, 25.17

πολλαπλάσιος 25.21

πολύς 1.11, [fr. 2.9], 2.27, 8.37, 9.36, 10.15, [12.30], 13.8, 13.20, 13.26, 14.3, 14.20, 14.22, 15.10, 15.14, 16.14, 17.4, 17.38, 18.17, 18.33, 18.38, 18.42, 19.12, 20.24, 20.42, 21.23, 21.47, 23.13, 24.31, 25.24, 25.36, 27.5, 27.34, 28.2

πολυτελής 28.7

πολυτέλια 23.45

πονεῖν 18.43

πονηρός 4.6, 10.21

πόνος fr. 2.6, 10.11, 13.13, 13.40, [13.42], 14.21, 14.31, 15.36, 16.27, 18.20, 18.45, 19.12, 19.21

πορίζειν 1.11, 1.13, 12.41, [13.42], 17.47, 20.25, 22.8, 23.2, 24.19, 26.46

πορισμός fr. 2.15, 14.15, 22.19

ποριστής 3a.9

ποριστικός 24.10

πόσις 9.33

πόσος 21.37

ποσός 9.41

ποτε 7.43, 11.18, 13.7, 13.43, 22.12, 22.33

που 13.17, 15.15

πρᾶγμα 3a.15, 13.6, 13.9, 13.31, 18.15, 21.21, 25.19, 25.48, 27.28, 27.38

πραγματεία 12.38, 22.14

πραγματικός 5.5

πρακτικός 22.32

πρᾶξις [2.29]

πρέπειν 14.10

πρίασθαι 25.29

προαιρεῖσθαι 12.15, 21.37

προϊστάναι 14.12, 20.39, 25.17

προκεῖσθαι 10.12

προλέγειν 1.20, 13.34, 16.21, 17.2, 20.12, 21.14, 25.32

προληπτικός 5.3

πρόληψις 20.9, 20.17, 20.27, 21.8

προνοεῖν 25.11

πρός + acc. [A.11], [B.1], [B.9], [B.16], fr. 2.15, 5.7, [7.10], 7.37, 9.11, 10.9, 11.39, 12.2, 12.13, 12.27, [12.29], 12.41, 13.37, 13.38, 14.3, 15.19, 15.36, 16.1, 16.7, 16.13, 16.31, [16.36], 16.38, 17.18, 17.35, 18.4, 18.21, 18.29, 18.35, 19.2, 19.8, 19.9, 19.21, 19.30, 21.20, 22.2, 22.7, 22.11, 22.39, 23.12, 24.37, 25.3, 26.9, 26.23, 27.44, [28.3]

πρός + dat. [7.10], 18.35

προσάγειν 16.12

προσαγορεύειν 5.1, 10.31

προσγίνεσθαι 25.37

προσδεῖν 4.26, 4.28, 5.12, 13.26

συνεργεῖν 14.3, 24.40
συνεργός 2.5
συνέχειν 22.9, 23.40
συνεχίζειν 25.30
συνήθεια 4.1, 4.32, 5.4, 20.4, 21.20
συνήθης 1.4, 1.17, 9.6, 10.30
σύνθεσις 26.11
συνιστάναι 2.19, 8.12, 8.16
συνοικία 23.19
συνοικονομεῖν 8.32
συνπαραλαμβάνειν 26.25
συνπαρέπεσθαι [13.1], 18.17
συντείνειν 22.40
συντελεῖν 7.14, 7.36, 22.46
σύντομος 12.4
σύντονος 17.34, 18.14
συντυχία 14.2
συστολή 26.7
σφαλερός 15.44
σχολάζειν 22.34
σῴζειν 15.28, 15.43, [16.26], 18.16, 18.27, 18.28, [18.39]
Σωκράτης 5.6, 5.16, 6.7, 6.11, 2.17
σῶμα 13.12
σωρεύειν 14.40
σωρευτός 16.42
σωτηρία 11.44 (Theophrastus), 16.17, 18.18, 18.30
σώφρων 6.2, 2.38, 15.46, [23.17]
ταλαιπωρία 18.15
ταλαίπωρος 11.30, 22.4, 23.7
ταμεῖον A.16
ταμίευμα 2.31
ταπεινός 16.2
τάττειν [A.19], 10.42
τάχα 11.24
ταχύς 15.29, 17.5, 19.6, 20.42, 25.29
τέκνον 27.9

τεκνοποιία 10.17
τελεῖν fr. 1.7
τέλειος [17.38]
τελευτᾶν 27.8
τέλος 13.4, 15.20, 17.45, 19.9, 22.42
τερθρεία 27.42
τερπνός 3a.15
τερπός 15.40
τέρψις 10.45, 18.47
τέτταρα 10.29
τέχνη 7.30, 8.8, 10.39, 21.45, [21.46], 23.21
τεχνίτης 17.3, 17.31
τηλικοῦτος 6.16, 16.13
τήρησις 14.10, 17.33, 23.38, 24.26, 26.31
τιθέναι 1.18, 6.18, 7.2, 19.15, 27.9
τιμή 9.29
τίμιος 25.27
τις 1.19, fr. 1.17, fr. 1.20, 3a.16, [2.0], 2.16, [7.10], 8.8, 8.9, 13.9, 13.13, 13.17, 13.34, 13.38, 13.43, 14.12, 14.18, [14.28], 14.37, 15.10, 16.22, 16.29, 17.7, 17.24, 17.30, 17.32, 17.38, 18.21, 18.37, 19.17, 19.20, 21.27, 22.7, 22.33, 24.9, 25.5, 25.6, 25.17, 26.12, 26.46, 27.13, 27.18, 27.21, 28.10
τίς [2.36], 8.13, 8.40, [8.46], 9.4, 9.8, [9.21], 10.7, 16.12, 17.40, 20.11, 21.38, 21.44, [21.45]
τοι [16.24]
τοιοῦτος 3a.18, 10.28, 12.27, 13.19, 14.2, 14.39, 15.16, 15.22, 15.27, 17.12, 17.14, 17.25, 17.30, 17.42, 18.38, 19.24, 19.29, 19.32, 19.33, 20.22, 20.33, 21.6, [22.2], 22.28, 25.2, 27.34, 28.10

124 PHILODEMUS, *ON PROPERTY MANAGEMENT*

τοίνυν 4.25, 7.46, 12.6, 12.26, 27.6
τόπος 12.28
τοσοῦτος [fr. 2.13], 5.29, 18.26
τότε 1.18
τραγῳδεῖν 7.18
τρέφειν 9.22, 10.19
τρίτος 23.23
τρόπος [B.12], fr. 1.21, fr. 2.14, 9.4, 14.11, 15.8
τροφή 8.29 (Theophrastus), 8.31, 8.33, 9.31, 9.46
τυγχάνειν 11.35
τύχειν 5.34, 16.11, 25.3
ὑβρίζειν 9.27
ὑβριστής 9.35
ὑγιαίνειν 13.12
ὑγίεια B.9, 11.39
ὑγιής 16.9
ὑγρός 27.2
ὑπακούειν fr. 1.18
ὕπαρξις 24.45, 25.23, 25.30
ὑπάρχειν [A.4], 3a.12, 8.27, 11.5, 8.15, 8.27 (Theophrastus), 11.5, 13.6, 13.10, [13.17], 13.18, 13.31, 16.20, 16.37, 16.43, 17.42, 18.25, 19.24, 19.37, 20.9, 20.44, 24.38, 27.6, 27.10
ὑπεῖναι 6.1
ὑπέρ + gen. 6.8, 8.18, 21.9, 21.15, 21.25, 21.30
ὑπερέχειν 7.43
ὑπέρμετρος 16.38
ὑπερορᾶν 25.22
ὑπεροχή 19.2, 27.45
ὑπηρέτης 19.25
ὕπνος 7.24
ὑπό + acc. 11.1
ὑπό + gen. 5.15, 5.16, 7.8, 7.11, 7.13, 8.36, 9.26, 10.1, 14.27,

[15.33], 16.4, 21.18, [21.47], 21.48, 24.22, 24.24
ὑπογράφειν 12.5
ὑπολαμβάνειν [1.3], 8.45
ὑπομένειν 15.35
ὑποτάττειν 12.14, 26.21
ὑστερεῖν 16.39
ὕστερον [B.4], 11.34
ὑφήγησις [2.22]
φαίνεσθαι 7.11, 11.19, 13.3, 14.6, 17.15, 17.30, 22.29, 27.29
φάναι 6.18, 9.17, 11.22, 20.32, 22.43, 27.38
φανερός 9.38, 9.40, 11.34
φάσκειν 8.38, 20.46
φαῦλος [21.33], [21.34]
φείδεσθαι 25.21, 27.7
φειδώ 27.12
φέρειν 20.26
φεύγειν 13.5, 13.30
φθείρειν 15.30
φθονεῖν 1.19
φιλάνθρωπος 18.34
φιλία 24.27
φιλονεικεῖν 15.17
φίλος 13.16, 15.6, 23.15, 24.42, 26.4, 26.9, 26.26, 27.5
φιλοσοφεῖν 20.46
φιλοσοφία B.10, 7.32, 11.40, 26.14
φιλόσοφος 2.10, 7.12, 7.34, 9.45, 11.16, 11.31, 11.42, 12.16, 12.18, 12.42, 23.25, 27.5, 27.16, 27.33
φιλοτιμία 4.14
φιλοχρήματος 11.4, 17.13
φοβεῖν 27.41
φόβος 23.42, 24.7
φρίκη 24.3
φροντίς 12.37, 13.3, 13.12, 13.32, 15.42, 18.24, 19.14, 19.21, 22.14

φροντιστής 17.33
φρουρός 11.42
φυγή 28.9
φύειν [7.35]
φυλακή [A.12], 11.21, 12.9, 12.24, 16.25, 17.29, 18.31, 18.42, 19.35, 28.4
φυλακτικός [10.33], 10.41, 24.10
φύλαξ 18.32
φυλάττειν 1.12, 10.2, 14.45, 19.11, 22.9, 24.19, 25.6, 26.47
φυσικός 5.8, 14.19, 16.3, 16.30, 17.44
φύσις 8.22, 8.40, 19.17
χαρίζεσθαι 26.3
χάριν 10.27, 15.20
χάρις 19.39
χειμάζειν 13.15
χείρων 10.18, 26.41
χορηγεῖν 9.43
χρεία 15.38, 16.23, 17.18, 17.26, 17.36
χρή [A.25], [B.2], 22.5, 26.1
χρῆμα 1.12, [fr. 1.4], [fr. 1.5], [3a.9], 3a.11, [4.27], 10.31, 12.8, 14.45, 16.18, 17.29, 18.44, 19.35, 20.40, 21.1, 28.5
χρηματίζεσθαι 20.13
χρηματισμός 2.5, 16.39, 17.8, 20.45
χρηματιστής 19.43, 20.10, 20.15, 20.18, 20.28, 21.10, 21.32, 21.33, 21.44
χρῆσθαι [A.13], fr. 2.16, 5.38, 8.9, 8.12, 10.3, 13.39, 14.9, 19.19, 19.47
χρήσιμος A.15, B.11, [B.14], 11.8, 11.10, 16.41, 17.12, 18.1, 26.16
χρῆσις 10.7, 20.7, 22.20, 26.29

χρηστικός [A.3], [10.34]
χρόνος 10.13, 26.12
χωρίς 9.3, 18.19
ψεῦδος 2.34
ψυχή 4.7
ὧδε 17.46
ὠνεῖσθαι [A.16], 11.23, 25.26
ὡς 6.1, 6.14, [2.20], [2.26], 2.27, 7.42, 9.41, 10.42, 12.6, 12.7, 12.44, 13.20, 13.33, 14.2, 14.18, 14.34, 15.8, 15.22, [17.19], 18.8, 18.47, 21.23, 21.34, 22.26, 23.29, 23.32, 23.45, 24.11, 24.41, 25.31, 25.38, 27.29
ὡσαύτως 19.40, 21.43
ὥσπερ [B.6], 8.31, 19.25, 20.7, 25.17, 25.42
ὥστε [A.24], 3a.6, 3a.28, 8.25 (Theophrastus), 9.8, 9.13, 11.19, 12.22, 15.34, 18.43, 22.32, 23.9, 24.6, 24.17, 24.27
ὠφελεῖν 3a.28, 27.29
ὠφελία 3a.5, [10.45], [20.48]
ὠφέλιμος 27.19

CPSIA information can be obtained at www.ICGtesting.com
Printed in the USA
LVOW06*0848010813

345701LV00001B/5/P

9 781589 837652